Becoming a Dig

MW00424123

Becoming a Digital Parent is a practical, readable guide that will help all parents have confidence to successfully navigate technology with their children. It accessibly presents evidence-based guidance to offer an overview of the digital landscape, empowering parents to embrace opportunities while keeping children responsible and safe online.

Covering a range of topics including developmental stages, screen time, bed time, gaming, digital identities, and helpful parenting apps and resources, Carrie Rogers-Whitehead explores the challenges and opportunities involved in parenting in the digital age. With advice for parents of babies through to teenagers, each chapter includes an explanation of the latest research, interviews with parents and experts, and helpful case studies gathered by the author during her extensive experience of working directly with parents and children. This book will show parents how to communicate better with their children, create a family technology plan, put in place intervention strategies when things happen, and take advantage of the benefits technology can afford us.

Becoming a Digital Parent is ideal for all parents looking to effectively navigate the technological world, and the range of professionals who work with them.

Carrie Rogers-Whitehead is the founder of Digital Respons-Ability, a mission-based company training thousands of parents, students, and educators on digital citizenship. She is the author of *Digital Citizenship: Teaching Strategies and Practice from the Field* and other academic works. Carrie is also a mother and continuously strives to be a better digital parent.

Becoming a Digital Parent

A Practical Guide to Help Families
Navigate Technology

Carrie Rogers-Whitehead

Routledge
Taylor & Francis Group

NEW YORK AND LONDON

First published 2021
by Routledge
52 Vanderbilt Avenue, New York, NY 10017

and by Routledge
2 Park Square, Milton Park, Abingdon, Oxon, OX14 4RN

Routledge is an imprint of the Taylor & Francis Group, an informa business

© 2021 Carrie Rogers-Whitehead

Library of Congress Cataloging-in-Publication Data
A catalog record for this book has been requested

ISBN: 978-0-367-42464-0 (hbk)
ISBN: 978-0-367-42462-6 (pbk)
ISBN: 978-0-367-82428-0 (ebk)

Typeset in Sabon
by Apex CoVantage, LLC

With love, for Kellen

Contents

Preface   ix

1   **Parenting Is Not What It Used to Be:**
    Technology Trends   1

    Brief History of Technology Since the 1970s 2
    Entertainment Trends and Technology 5
    WiFi 10

2   **Prevention Science and Technology**   14

    Prevention Science 15
    Focus on the Cause, Not the Symptom 21

3   **Generation Alpha: Parenting Around Tech**
    in Young Children   25

    Developmental Stages 27
    Technology Impacts on Language and Social
       Development 31
    Tech Trends for Generation Alpha 33
    Creating Technology Norms at Home 39
    Conversation Starters for Children Ages 0–8 41

4   **The Tween Years: Puberty + Peers + Tech**   45

    Puberty 46
    Tween Trends Online 49

First Phones and Social Media Accounts 52
Setting Boundaries 56
Conversation Starters for Children Ages 8–13 59

5   **Digital Identities: Teens and Technology**   62

Teen Development 64
Sex and the Digital World 66
Teen Mental Health and Technology 77
Digital Branding 84
Strategies for Communicating With Your Teen 89

6   **Screen Time: The Real Facts and Research**   95

Research on Screen Time 95
Sleep and Screens 102
*Strategies and Suggestions for Family Screen
    Time Issues 108*

7   **Gaming: A Potential Pitfall or Positive**   114

Debunking Myths About Gaming 114
Concerns About Gaming 119
Benefits of Gaming 133
Parenting Strategies and Norms for Gaming 136

8   **Resources and Apps: What to Use at Different
    Developmental Stages**   143

Ratings and Labels 143
Technology for Children Ages 0–8 147
Technology for Children Ages 8–13 151
Technology for Teens Ages 13–18 158
Resources for Parents 161

*Appendix: Conversation Starters and Questions
    to Ask a Child About Technology*   168
Resources   176
Index   190

Preface

When I founded Digital Respons-Ability, we first only taught students. We would go into classrooms and meet week after week with students talking about digital health, screen time, privacy, media, and much more. In those classes we would talk to and survey the students about what they thought of social media, technology, their own usage—and the students were saying different things than the adults.

The majority of our teens did not see as many issues with their screen time or social media use, unlike the parents. While an adult saw a meme as offensive or dumb, the teen would laugh. Kids were having fun on games, while adults attended conferences and classes discussing gaming addiction. This disconnect became more evident to me over time and I realized: I've got to teach both groups.

While teaching parents I found that many were afraid. This was new and unfamiliar. Their kids were talking about things they didn't know about and they felt their kids were tuning them out to be behind a screen. They had read media reports and heard scary stories. They had watched speakers and influencers who spoke in hyperbole and cherry-picked research. They would get conflicting advice from well-meaning people.

I wanted to help those parents—and I wanted to help myself. This book came from my experiences teaching *and* my experiences parenting. While writing this book my child turned eight years old and technology was more present in his life. I know puberty is just around the corner. I know that very soon he will ask for his first phone. I know that in a few short years he will be developing his own digital identity. And I know that while I advise families and teach on this topic, parenting your own child is different. It's far easier to give advice than to take it.

Perhaps you're reading this because you're unfamiliar. Or you're like me and you feel educated on the topic. In either case, you'll learn something new. And along with learning new things, hopefully you'll walk away with less fear. For example, the process of researching, interviewing, and writing Chapter 7 on gaming helped calm my anxieties. Gaming is a big interest of children. I had attended conference presentations on the perils of gaming and while I played games as a kid, I was unfamiliar with the new landscape. From researching, talking, and being open to new concepts, most of my reservations about gaming are gone.

Children are constantly changing, and so is the world. The COVID-19 pandemic burst on the scene while writing this book, shifting education and greatly increasing our time behind screens. Since the pandemic is still happening, it's impossible to know the long-term effects. But I am pretty sure if I wrote this book again in a year, Chapter 6 on screen time would be different.

I'm interested to see what changes come next. But while there is uncertainty, I am certain the basic principles of parenting, loving your child and taking care of their needs, remain the same. When I teach parents, I tell them that the fact that they are in my class demonstrates that they care. Showing up is more important than knowing all the different apps, stats, and devices. You showed up by picking up this book and you're well on your way to becoming a digital parent.

Chapter 1

Parenting Is Not What It Used to Be

Technology Trends

When I was in junior high, I was convinced that the Internet was never going to take off. This was actually something I said to my friend, as we sat in the computer room doing homework. We were researching for a group project in history and had tried in vain to look things up online.

The big, boxy computer took about fifteen minutes to boot up. We had to wait while it made alien beeps and screeches, hoping we wouldn't get some weird black or blue screen and it actually came on. If we were lucky, the big grey behemoth would bring us to a desktop with Netscape, and my favorite pastime while waiting for things to load: Minesweeper.

At this point, I needed to alert everyone else in the house that we were going online. I would clomp down the stairs and yell, "Mom, don't get on the phone. I'm getting on the computer." Then, I would clomp back up and cross my fingers she heard me, nothing came up for which she needed to use the phone, or no one called the house. I would also hold my breath that my little sister would not come into the room wanting to get on the computer, because there was only one in the whole house and it was dedicated to homework. Getting online was a fraught process.

If I were lucky enough and everything worked out, I would click on Netscape, but very carefully. I knew if I clicked too much, it would throw off the computer. It would think I wanted multiple screens, and then I might have to restart the computer and start all over. Back then, I was also very careful on whatever I clicked on, because an innocent click on an article or picture would be a five-minute detour while the screen loaded. I was extremely deliberate. Browsing wasn't really a thing in junior high. I had to log on, do what I needed to do, and then log off.

That afternoon with my friend, we had finally given up on the computer and loaded up a CD-ROM, Encarta, which was much more reliable than this Internet thing everyone kept talking about. After poor loading speeds, bad links, and holding our breath that everything would align, and we could actually get online, we gave up. Exasperated, I said, "I don't know why anyone would want to use the Internet."

That is the Internet parents of Gen Zs and Alphas are familiar with. The painstakingly slow, dial-up kind. While I had Internet through junior high and high school, it was not a big part of my life. When I was older, I would chat on it and sometimes play games, but it was a tool, like a dishwasher.

I got a phone my junior year, a gray and black Nokia. But like the Internet, it was functional. It would sit in my purse or car most of the time and only come up when I was working late, or plans changed. Texting was still very expensive and very few people did it. Besides making calls, the only other thing I would do on that Nokia was play Snake.

The technology of older Millennials and Gen X may as well be from a different planet as far as Gen Z is concerned. The concept of loading in a disc, not texting, only having one computer, and slow loading speeds is something that they have never experienced. If the Internet stayed at that mid-1990s level, my tween self would be right. Why *would* anyone use an Internet like that? But that is no longer the case. And my childhood experiences with technology are radically different than what my child will experience.

Technology is not the same; it's radically different. However, we create policies, rules, and norms in our homes, schools, and organizations as if it were the same. We are often in the *computer room* mindset, that if we just limit devices at home, then any issues are taken care of. But there are no computer rooms with one shared bulky device anymore. In some cases, the whole house is a computer. The Internet is not confined to one device or place. It's everywhere. But with filters, restrictions, blocks, and rules, we act as if it were. This chapter will cover tech trends into the near future. If we want to parent effectively, we need to understand this new reality. Things are not the same, and they won't be again.

Brief History of Technology Since the 1970s

Microprocessors, Atari, Nintendo, fiber optics, VHS, Walkmans, and much more came out in the 1970s and 1980s. These decades, particularly the 1970s, contributed to the exponential growth of computing and modern technology. Still, much of this tech was more a novelty than a commodity. Most video gaming still took place in an arcade, video rentals in a store, and computing in certain fields of work. While children of the 1970s and 1980s, Generation X and some Millennials, had interactions with technology, it was not a constant in their lives. A big reason it was not integrated in every aspect of life is that there was no Internet. The Internet is the glue that connected music, gaming, entertainment, and computing all together, for good or ill.

In 1995, Robert Metcalf, the individual credited with inventing Ethernet, made a notorious prediction. "Almost all of the many predictions now being made about 1996 hinge on the Internet's continuing exponential growth. But I predict the Internet will soon go spectacularly supernova and in 1996 catastrophically collapse" (Townsend, 2016). You may chuckle now at that statement, which Metcalf has gone on record to deeply regret, but many people, my tween self included, believed it. The Internet was slow and not very searchable. Computer Associates founder Charles Wang was deeply skeptical. He told the *New York Times*, "Put newspapers and magazines out of business? It will never happen. . . . People say the Internet will replace stores. It will never happen" (Townsend, 2016). But it did happen, and it happened quickly.

From its time as ARPANET in the 1960s and 1970s, used by governments and researchers, the Internet started commercialization in the early 1980s. It was not officially called the Internet until 1995 when the Federal Networking Council adopted that term. In 1990, there was the World Wide Web, introduced by Tim Berners-Lee. While the World Wide Web and Internet are used interchangeably, the Web is a service that travels over the Internet through hypertext.

Higher-speed access was not available to the public until 1996, but even then, it was very limited. It wasn't until the late 1990s and early 2000s that broadband instead of dial-up became the means of Internet access. Broadband access has increased exponentially. As of 2017, the Federal Communications Commission (FCC) reported 92.3% of Americans have broadband access at home (FCC, 2019). The Internet that young people are familiar with is only about ten to fifteen years old. Broadband access and the growth of the Internet led to the next revolution and evolution of tech: mobile.

Smartphones

Almost all teens have a smartphone. A 2018 Pew Research study reports that 95% of teens can access one (Anderson and Jiang, 2018). Consider how quickly this has happened. IBM technically made a smartphone in the mid-Nineties, but it was bulky and only used in very limited fashion before being put aside. The infrastructure wasn't there to support it. While the Internet was available, it wasn't until the mid 2000s that 3G technology had improved to the point to make it worthwhile to connect through mobile. While Apple may want to claim all the credit for the innovation of the iPhone, the path was laid out a decade in advance. This allowed Steve Jobs to stride across the Macworld stage in his famous black turtleneck on January 9, 2007, and introduce the iPhone. In just eleven years, a novelty item had become part of almost every adolescent's life.

A big innovation Apple *can* claim most of the credit for is popularizing apps. An app is a software application. The Snake game I played as a teen on my Nokia phone was one of the first apps. At first, Steve Jobs only wanted Apple to develop apps, not any third parties. Due to convincing by the Apple staff, Jobs eventually changed his mind and allowed others to create apps for the iPhone, but not without giving Apple a 30% cut. This encouraged the app

Figure 1.1 Smartphone with apps

revolution to happen. Small companies, as well as large, could have access to millions of eyes on smartphones.

Apps are what make a smartphone a smartphone. They also contribute to an increasing amount of screen time. Statistica estimates the total app downloads will leap to 352 billion in 2021. That's up from about 200 billion in 2017, which already was a jump from 2016 when there were about 149 billion app downloads (Clement, 2020). These numbers far exceed the number of people on the planet. If every person on the planet had a smartphone, they would need to download at least three apps to reach those 2017 numbers.

Whose eyes are on these apps? Unsurprisingly, it's Generation Z. A company that measures cross-platform tech statistics, Comscore, reports that the ages 18–24 report the most time on these apps, close to 100 hours each month. These are your children, students in classrooms now, and those who in a decade or less will come to dominate the workforce.

Entertainment Trends and Technology

TV Trends

Other revolutions happened in entertainment. A child of the 1970s through the 1990s probably remembers watching the clock closely for when their favorite television show started. You may have set the timer on your VCR to record or read the *TV Guide* or local newspaper on the day's programming.

I remember in elementary school, my neighbor friends and I counted down the hours until Saturday night. That's when SNICK happened. SNICK stood for Saturday Night Nickelodeon. It had such amazing shows as *Are You Afraid of the Dark?*, *The Ren and Stimpy Show*, and *The Secret World of Alex Mack*. We would gather our popcorn, blankets, and soda and hurry to get settled before the first show started. When commercials came on, there would be a mad dash to the bathroom or to the kitchen. There weren't any pause buttons back then. You could not wait until later to watch your favorite show. You scheduled your day around it, and if you missed it, you'd be that kid at school the next day who didn't know what everyone else was talking about.

TV now, like the Internet, is ubiquitous and constant. If you're feeling as if there's too much TV—you're right. The number of new original series that debuted in 2018 was the highest on record.

There were 495 scripted original series on TV, which includes basic and paid cable, online services, and broadcast TV. This is an 85% increase from 2011. And before the 2010s there were even fewer shows, only 182 in 2002 (Hibberd, 2018).

As broadband speeds increased, streaming services became possible. The most well-known is Netflix, which was founded in 1997. It originally only sold or rented DVDs. It wasn't until 2007, the same year that the iPhone debuted, that it started streaming media. In 2012, Netflix started creating original content, which bumped up that increase of new content even more. Netflix is not the only subscription service. Amazon Prime Video is close behind in popularity. It carved a similar path as Netflix, launching in 2006 primarily with video, but then adding their own original content in 2013.

Streaming is another *new normal* for Generation Z and younger. The concept of waiting for a show and scheduling your day around it is gone. The phenomenon of a record number of people watching a show at once is gone. TV is more diverse and fragmented than ever before. Scripted TV used to reach large segments of people, like the very famous last episode of *M*A*S*H* in 1983, which had almost 106 million viewers. Almost all programming that has received those numbers since the 2010s has been sporting events.

The growth of new TV content has allowed new voices, perspectives, and cultures to get screen time they may have not had before. On the other hand, having so many different types of programming provides less common ground. The choice of content can provide new perspectives or allow someone to wall himself off. The magnitude of choices can also create fatigue and anxiety. The long list of shows on people's watch lists, or never feeling as though they can keep up, can make TV feel more like a chore than entertainment.

Music Trends

When I was in high school, Napster was in its heyday. Napster highlighted the Wild West of the early Internet. In the late 1990s, two teens developed the technology—allowing Internet users to go into each other's hard drives and share their MP3 music files. The MP3 was a relatively new invention, coming out just a few years prior. The tech behind this file format allowed a huge reduction in file sizes, which was vital during the mid and late 1990s when dial-up was the standard for connecting online.

I remember booting up my old Sony laptop and opening up Napster to the world's music collection. I spent more time browsing what was available than actually downloading; it was still a hefty time commitment to download and then burn a CD. But during that browsing I found artists and music I would never have discovered without the short-lived file-sharing service.

Before Napster, buying music was more complicated. And while I was choosy with what files I would download, I was much choosier when deciding where to spend my hard-earned high school job cash. Like walking into a brightly-lit Blockbuster, going into Sam Goody with its wall-to-wall selection of CDs could be overwhelming. There were so many choices, but only so much cash.

Napster didn't just give young adults music, it revolutionized the Internet. From *Downloaded*, the documentary of Napster which came out in 2013, director Alex Winter talked about that time. "There was no ramp up. There was no transition. . . . Napster was a ridiculous leap forward" (Lamont, 2013). That leap forward benefited many later Internet companies. It showed that people wanted music, and if they had to wait six hours to download it, they would. This paved the way for streaming music services, first with iTunes, then Spotify and Pandora. Facebook, Dropbox, and other companies have also built off the file-sharing tech of Napster.

Napster also changed the music industry. Younger generations have much more choice than any Sam Goody store. This choice has flattened some music sales but allowed more independent voices. Digital music has also changed the music landscape. The idea of a concept album, tying in different tracks in one cohesive vision, has less relevancy when singles by different artists are played one after another. Musicians write music for singles, not albums.

Young people live in a different music landscape with constant availability and choice. Now they can curate their own soundtracks and favorites with a click of a button. And they can discover artists much more easily than browsing metal racks of CDs. Younger generations have quickly adopted streaming. According to a report by Statista, there is a "steep drop-off in usage from the age of 55" (Richter, 2015). But unlike owning an LP, cassette, or CD, you don't own a streaming service. This may mean more a fickle relationship between an album, artist, and the listener.

And streaming services have not shown large profits. The number one music company in 2018 was Spotify, but despite having over a billion dollars in revenue, it keeps losing money (Jenkins, 2018). Artists lose money too, making fractions of a penny from downloads. While the music industry has democratized and allowed diversity, it hasn't really provided revenue, except to very few. Digital music and its various mediums will continue to evolve, but like TV, a few short years have upended all the traditional models.

Videogaming

From the pixels on an Atari screen to immersive reality, gaming has made a huge technological shift in the last thirty years. Your children are probably gaming. Statista reports that over half of regular gamers are under 35, with about a third of those under 18 (Gough, 2019). Videogaming and the effects on families will be discussed in greater detail in Chapter 7. For now, take a minute to see how rapidly it has changed since the 1970s.

As with TV and music, a big change in gaming is moving from the physical to the digital. In 2016, gaming turned a corner, with most being sold digitally instead of physically (Mediakix, 2019). Not only the medium of gaming has changed, but the model. Companies are shifting to a digital subscription model. Instead of buying an individual game, subscribers purchase a monthly plan with a certain number of downloads.

A driving factor behind the subscription model is Steam. Developed by the Valve corporation, Steam offers servers, support, and digital rights management for PC gaming. Consider it like Google Play for PC games. The thought behind Steam and other subscription-based gaming is that players do not purchase games based on the company that released it; rather they buy the game. This allows companies to push out updates more quickly and make extra income from expansion packs, loot boxes, or other add-ons. In the past when a player would buy a new game, everything about that game came packed in a plastic case. Now players purchase a code they input online, and if they want more, they must pay to play.

I had an NES (Nintendo Entertainment System) as a child. Like many others around the world, I played *Super Mario Brothers*, *Contra*, *Donkey Kong*, and many more classics. I enjoyed playing them, but they were taken out, booted up, and then finished. They were something you did for a few hours one afternoon, before you went outside to jump on the trampoline. These games had a clear beginning and end. Once you finished the game, you were done.

With streaming and subscription models, the games never end. Video games are also fundamentally different than in the 1970s and 1980s. They tell stories. Writing in game website Polygon, Colin Campbell describes this shift (Campbell, 2019):

> The dichotomy of story and not-story is at the center of gaming history. In the early days of games, those beeping, menacing Space Invaders arrived without any apparent motivation, inner conflict, or backup plan. We just shot them, and they shot us, and everyone was happy. The action game was born. . . .
>
> Over the next three decades, these entirely different forms came together, and action games began to include narrative elements. Role-playing adventures, the descendants of those text adventures, became action-oriented exercises, interspersing killing and fighting with cutscenes or walking conversations between characters.

These types of games include the international hit *World of Warcraft*, role-playing games like *Final Fantasy* or *Assassins Creed*, and other open-world or sandbox-style games like *Minecraft* or *Animal Crossing*.

This shift is exciting; people can enjoy better graphics, game play, and stories. But they also spend more hours behind a screen. A better way to look at it is that people don't really play games, the games play them. The player becomes immersed in a new world, which can be hard to put away for the sometimes-dull real one.

In addition to more narrative and open-world games, eSports have had a huge growth in the last five years (Perez, 2018). Also known as electronic sports, they involve organized multi-player video game competitions, often between professional players. There have always been video game competitions, but since the 2010s, they've become big business, reaching billions of dollars in revenue (Rovell, 2016). Fans of eSports spend money on their favorite players and leagues, just like professional sports. Statista estimates that per capita, eSports spending will exceed five billion dollars in 2020, up from about 3.5 billion in 2017 (Gough, 2017).

Professional eSports players can make over a million dollars and large stadiums sell out for spectators to watch these players battle it out. A generation ago parents may have told their kids, "Video games are a waste of time. Find something to do that makes you money." That's no longer necessarily the case. Those old sayings and beliefs about video games need to be updated. Video games are no longer something we play at an arcade, or for a few hours after school; they've increasingly become a part of everyday life. With games constantly in our back pockets on a mobile device and at home, and streaming on Twitch and YouTube, we're surrounded by games.

WiFi

How many Internet-connected devices do you have at home? Now think, how many Internet devices do you have on your person? That number of Internet-connected devices per person is growing. Research with *Business Insider* suggests that for each person on Earth there will be more than four devices. Much of this is spurred by the Internet of Things (IoT) growth—Internet-connected objects beyond traditional computers (Intelligence, 2016). This can include a smartwatch, a smart speaker, and refrigerators that tell you when to order more milk.

To keep up with this growth, 5G technology is expanding. 5G is a new cellular standard, an upgrade from 4G which came about ten years ago. This 5G access works at a higher spectrum, above 60 GHz. A big reason 5G has been developed is to upgrade existing networks. As more devices and users need Internet access, the current bandwidth can get crowded. 5G will first be implemented at those stadiums where eSports fans gather, and other places with a concentrated group of people. 5G will eventually open other frequencies to minimize delays and give much faster speed. Consumers will need new phones and data plans to utilize the 5G standard.

5G is a far cry from the early days of WiFi, which is a big leap from dial-up Internet. 5G can literally download a movie in seconds. Unlike dial-up, which uses your phone line and a modem to connect, WiFi utilizes radio waves to provide connectivity through wireless adaptors that can connect to a router. Dial-up speeds can go up to 56,000 bytes per second, compared to traditional broadband, which can provide millions of bytes per second (IEEE, 2019). It's basically the difference between riding a tricycle and a rocket. WiFi was initially developed in the late 1990s and approved for home use in 1999. While WiFi continued to improve since the late 1990s, it wasn't until 2009 and improved efficiency with multiple antennas that allowed increases in data without a need for more power or bandwidth. This coincided with the growth of streaming services, which would not have been possible with slower data transmission speeds.

WiFi continues to evolve, and the next iteration may be Li-Fi. Li-Fi is a completely different type of transmission to WiFi. WiFi works through radio waves while Li-Fi transmits signals through light. Light waves are over 100 times faster than radio waves. So, the potential for (literal) lightning-fast speeds is a possibility. Pilot projects have been tested since 2015 but Li-Fi is not a commercially viable solution yet (Revolutionary, 2019).

The Internet of a generation ago, the one of parents now, is fundamentally different. One day I will struggle to explain to my son that there was only one computer, and we could only have one person using it at a time because it was connected to a phone line. What's a phone line, you ask? Well, let me back up a bit. . . .

The idea of waiting for a connection or loading times, or even waiting for a turn on the Internet, is already foreign to Generation Z and Alphas. In the near future, the concept of *connecting* to the Internet will also be foreign. The Internet will be ubiquitous, constant, and accessible everywhere. We had the Internet as children, but it was not the same Internet our children have.

If parents are making rules at home based on the "computer room" of their childhood, they are making false assumptions. Banning devices is not simple if WiFi or even Li-Fi is a constant presence. How can you limit access when it's streaming incredibly faster everywhere you go? How can you limit devices if everyone owns four? How do you tell someone to put away a game if the game never ends? How do parents communicate with different perspectives, norms, and definitions of entertainment and technology?

Parents must accept that access is fundamentally different, and what may have worked in 2005 did not work in 2015 and certainly will not in 2025. This is not easy, but hopefully parents can have some small comfort in knowing that their children will be battling the same issues when they become parents. This book hopes to make parenting around tech easier and will dive into these tech trends in the subsequent chapters. The first step, though, is to accept that what may have worked around technology when you were a kid is no longer relevant.

Summary Points: Technology Trends

- Technology has changed rapidly since the 1970s and there is a technology generation gap between parents and their children.
- Almost all teens own a smartphone and smartphone adoption since 2007 has been exponential.
- Generation Z spends more time on apps than previous generations.
- Streaming TV is the new normal for Generation Z and younger.
- Younger generations have quickly adopted the streaming music model.
- Gaming has had wide adoption and growth. A third of those under 18 are regular gamers.
- eSports is a multi-billion dollar growing industry with many young participants and fans.
- 5G is a new cellular standard which is creating even faster internet speeds. WiFi is significantly faster than dial-up, the Internet speed today's parents may have grown up with.
- Technology changes mean parents need to adapt their norms and parenting styles with their children.

References

Anderson, Monica, and Jingjing Jiang. "Teens, Social Media & Technology 2018." *Pew Research Center.* Pew Research Center: Internet, Science & Tech, May 30, 2020. www.pewresearch.org/internet/2018/05/31/teens-social-media-technology-2018/#vast-majority-of-teens-have-access-to-a-home-computer-or-smartphone.

Campbell, Colin. "How to Write a Video Game Story." *Polygon.* Polygon, January 10, 2019. www.polygon.com/features/2019/1/10/18165611/how-to-write-a-video-game-story-narrative-building-tips.

Clement, J. "Annual Number of Mobile App Downloads Worldwide 2019." January 17, 2020. www.statista.com/statistics/271644/worldwide-free-and-paid-mobile-app-store-downloads/ (Accessed June 2, 2020).

Gough, Christina. "Global Consumer Spend on eSports 2020." *Statista,* April 4, 2017. www.statista.com/statistics/691794/consumer-esports-spend/.

Gough, Christina. "U.S. Average Age of Video Gamers 2019." *Statista,* September 18, 2019. www.statista.com/statistics/189582/age-of-us-video-game-players-since-2010/.

Hibberd, James. "If You Think 2018 Had Too Many TV Shows, Here's Why." *EW.com.* https://ew.com/tv/2018/12/13/number-tv-shows-2018/ (Accessed January 11, 2019).

"IEEE Spectrum: Technology, Engineering, and Science News." https://spectrum.ieee.org/video/telecom/wireless/everything-you-need-to-know-about-5g (Accessed January 11, 2019).

Intelligence, Business Insider. "There Will Be 24 Billion IoT Devices Installed on Earth by 2020." *Business Insider.* Business Insider, June 9, 2016. www.businessinsider.com/there-will-be-34-billion-iot-devices-installed-on-earth-by-2020-2016-5.

"Internet Access Services Reports." *Federal Communications Commission,* September 20, 2019. www.fcc.gov/internet-access-services-reports.

Jenkins, Aric. "Spotify: Nevermind Profits." *Fortune,* May 30, 2018. http://fortune.com/2018/05/30/spotify-ipo-profit/.

Lamont, Tom. "Napster: The Day the Music Was Set Free." *The Guardian.* Guardian News and Media, February 24, 2013. www.theguardian.com/music/2013/feb/24/napster-music-free-file-sharing.

Perez, Matt. "Report: Esports to Grow Substantially and Near Billion-Dollar Revenues in 2018." *Forbes,* February 21, 2018. www.forbes.com/sites/mattperez/2018/02/21/report-esports-to-grow-substantially-and-near-a-billion-dollar-revenues-in-2018/#dac91e52b019.

"Revolutionary Wireless Communication Technology." April 20, 2019. https://lifi.co/ (Accessed June 2, 2020).

Richter, Felix. "Infographic: The Generation Gap in Music Streaming Adoption." *Statista Infographics,* March 16, 2015. www.statista.com/chart/3313/music-streaming-generation-gap/.

Rovell, Darren. "427 Million People Will Be Watching Esports by 2019, Reports Newzoo." *ESPN.* ESPN Internet Ventures, May 11, 2016. www.espn.com/esports/story/_/id/15508214/427-million-people-watching-esports-2019-reports-newzoo.

"The $50B Mobile Gaming Industry: Statistics, Revenue [Infographic]." *Mediakix,* July 28, 2019. http://mediakix.com/2018/03/mobile-gaming-industry-statistics-market-revenue/#gs.ipdCeKs.

Townsend, Tess. "What Bill Gates Got Wrong about the Internet in the 1990s." *Inc.com,* July 1, 2016. www.inc.com/tess-townsend/what-bill-gates-got-wrong-about-the-internet-in-the-1990s.html.

Chapter 2

Prevention Science and Technology

Humans have a desperate need to understand WHY. When something traumatic happens, we want to immediately understand why. For example, aboard every plane is a flight recorder, also called a black box. This object, actually a bright orange color, can aid in the understanding of a crash. It records conversations of the pilots and air traffic control and gives vital pieces of information to understand exactly what happened. We find the idea of a black box comforting—it gives answers. But if we examine air crashes and aviation more deeply, we realize that the black box only gives a piece of the puzzle. It cannot track the airplane over an ocean, it cannot pick up all the sounds and conversations from inside the plane, and it only gives clues about motivations and internal thoughts of pilots or others on the plane.

Plane crashes are caused by many variables beyond our control. Weather, malfunctions, air pressure, pilot fatigue, and even political motivations can mean the death of passengers. And although it's a sobering thought, sometimes there is nothing we can do. The crash is outside our control. Planes are complicated. Humans are even more complicated.

There is no human equivalent of a black box, but we like to think there is. We believe if we can hear recordings, read writings, talk to the person, and observe them, we can truly understand someone's behavior. But like a black box, these data points only provide glimpses. Although we don't think to think about it, human behavior is hard to predict. There are even more variables than with an airplane: upbringing, class, race, gender, sexuality, education, media consumption, peers, genetics, and many more.

Our behavior is motivated by many factors—but when violence or something fearful happens we want to home in on one factor.

We make assumptions and ascribe the problem to the individual or other concrete factors.

"He was a cyberbully because he was insecure."
"She acted that way because she's jealous."
"She was suicidal because of social media."
"He was cruel online because he didn't have good parents."
"She won't get off video games because games are addicting."

These simplified beliefs are comforting. They narrow down the infinite variables and randomness down to one clear answer. We cling to those beliefs because we feel we have more control.

"If bullying is simple a problem because of insecurities we should have a pep rally and tell everyone they're awesome!"
"Obviously I can't get off video games because I'm addicted. I'm not in control. It's not my fault."
"I don't have to worry about my kids ever having mental health issues because I don't let them on social media."

We believe we can 100% prevent the plane crash or prevent our child from ever being hurt online. Now, we do have control; behavior is certainly not totally random. Environmental factors, like the influence of a parent, are important. But it is more complicated than we like to believe.

If we blame the technology, if we latch onto the simple answer, we don't get closer to the real answers. We won't truly understand the crash, the behavior, the violence, the fear unless we dig deeper—unless we understand that technology is just one piece of the puzzle, just one clue for behavior.

This chapter will encourage you to not leap to conclusions about technology, to understand that there are many factors in your child's behavior. By examining multiple variables, you can parent with more empathy and nuance. Resist the urge to blame the technology. It's just one variable in the complicated black box that is a human.

Prevention Science

Prevention science is a multidisciplinary methodology that works to lessen or prevent dysfunctional human behavior. This methodology is used in disciplines such as public health, behavioral health, psychology, neurobiological sciences, mental health, and substance abuse treatments. This framework is used in this book and in the curriculum and classes I teach to students and parents. Prevention science has decades of research behind it; and it can help us understand digital behaviors as well as those in real life (Wilkins et al., 2014).

In prevention science there are risk factors and protective factors. A risk factor is a potential cause of dysfunctional behavior. For example, a child who is cyberbullied is more likely to cyberbully. Thus, being cyberbullied is a risk factor for cyberbullying (Rogers-Whitehead, 2018).

The opposite of a risk factor is a protective factor. This is something that can inhibit or stop the hurtful behavior from occurring. If a child has a positive and supportive peer group, that is a protective factor to not cyberbully others. In this book, some of the strategies and practices will be discussed through the framework of risk and protective factors (StopBullying.gov, 2019).

Think of a risk factor as a WHY for the behavior. A risk factor for a plane crashing is bad weather. Bad weather does not mean the plane will crash, but that it's more likely to. Another risk factor for a plane crash is equipment malfunction. When there are multiple risk factors, like bad weather and equipment malfunction, it's even more likely for the plane to crash. We cannot predict with 100% certainty that the plane will or will not crash, but we can examine those risk factors and make a better prediction—and decide we definitely aren't getting on the plane.

Dr. James DiPerna is the Director of the Penn State School Psychology Program and is a researcher into social emotional learning. He uses the prevention science construct in his work. "Prevention science particularly in early childhood settings is critical," he said. "The idea that we can actively prevent difficulties and challenges both from a student standpoint and a system standpoint is essential" (Rogers-Whitehead, 2020, interview with James DiPerna).

One hundred percent prevention is impossible. People are complicated and there are multitudes of risk factors and situations that individuals find themselves in. There is no foolproof method for behavioral change. People don't work like algorithms in which input equals output. However, prevention science provides us a framework to get as close to that 100% prevention as possible.

Social Emotional Learning and Prevention

Social emotional learning, referred to as SEL in education circles, is a preventative factor for unhealthy attitudes and behavior. CASEL, the Collaboration for Academic, Social, and Emotional Learning, defines SEL as "the process through which children and adults understand and manage emotions, set and achieve positive goals, feel and show empathy for others, establish and maintain positive relationships, and make responsible decisions"(CASEL, 2020). CASEL reported the positive effects of SEL in a meta-analysis in 2017 of over 2,013 SEL programs published in the *Journal of Child Development*. The researchers found that over three years after the SEL programs, students measured an average of thirteen points higher academically compared to their peers. The meta-analysis found that conduct problems, emotional distress, and drug use "were all significantly lower for students exposed to SEL programs" (CASEL, 2020).

While there are tech solutions to problematic behaviors around tech in this book, most of the suggestions revolve around SEL skills like emotional regulation, ability to set goals, self-efficacy, awareness of emotions, empathy, and more.

Dr. DiPerna suggests parents can encourage these SEL skills through "small moments." That means finding teachable moments throughout the day: on a drive, while cooking dinner, reading a story, shopping, and more. DiPerna suggests some of those lessons in small moments include how to get along, how to handle failure when things don't go your way. Those skills are some we're trying to promote long term for kids. I think a lot of times there are opportunities throughout any given day to draw attention to them, to praise kids when they do those things, or look for opportunities when they aren't doing those things as teachable moments. (Rogers-Whitehead, 2020, interview with James DiPerna)

Technology can provide its own teachable moments. Parents can comment on a game, TV show, or YouTube video and point out ideas and values.

One SEL skill mentioned several times in this book is self-regulation. DiPerna comments, I think self-regulation is an excellent one. . . . It's a skill area that's so fundamental and cuts across so many things that we do, and kids do. The ability to self-regulate, to recognize when you've done enough . . . being able to delay gratification. (Rogers-Whitehead, 2020, interview with James DiPerna)

These are important skills digital parents should encourage in their children and in themselves. Technology poses a particular difficulty related to self-regulation. There is constant content and entertainment. It can be hard to turn things off. Gaming, discussed in depth in Chapter 7, also calls for a high degree of self-regulation. DiPerna cites "being able to persevere" as another vital SEL skill and a skill needed to succeed in many games. "It's a fine line between sticking with something and sticking with it to the point where it becomes a problem and it undermines these certain skills and life outcomes" (Rogers-Whitehead, 2020, interview with James DiPerna). Parents are needed to help find that fine line between working hard and persevering and obsession, which can limit and cause harm emotionally and socially.

Prevention Programs That Don't Work

If we don't address the risk factors, we aren't addressing the WHY, and we aren't really touching on the problem. In the plane example, if there is old equipment and we decide to give the plane a fresh coat of paint, we are missing the problem. Now the plane may look better with its new paint job, but it's not actually helping anything. So often when schools, community organizations, and others want to prevent violence or other dysfunctions, we just give them a fresh coat of paint. It may look good from the outside, but it doesn't really make an impact. More problematically, we are ignoring the real problems and allowing them to get worse by only focusing on the surface.

One notorious program that doesn't address risk factors is D.A.R.E.: Drug Abuse Resistance Education. This program started in the 1980s and became the model for many school districts to prevent substance abuse. Trained police officers went into classrooms and talked about the dangers of substances available and advised children to "just say no" (Lilienfeld, 2014).

Meta-analyses of the D.A.R.E. program found that it may have had a negative impact. Some studies found that students were led to believe tobacco products weren't as bad when compared to other substances like cocaine or meth (Lilienfeld, 2014). The program also didn't address the WHYs of when young people use substances. They use those substances because of mental health concerns, bad parental modeling, abuse, and more. They did not typically start drinking or using drugs because they were unable to "just say no."

Christopher Ferguson is a professor of psychology at Stetson University who has conducted research on youth violence, video games, technology, and more. He uses a prevention science framework in his research and said:

> D.A.R.E. is terrible. It's intuitive for old people. Even worse than D.A.R.E is Scared Straight; I refer to that as porn for old people. Teenage kids getting screamed at is something that old people like but with a little critical thinking you can figure out why this may not be helpful.
>
> (Rogers-Whitehead, 2020, interview with Christopher Ferguson)

Scared Straight is a program in which young people are taken to confront former gang members and addicts. It was named after a 1978 documentary in which a group of juvenile offenders were filmed with convicts serving life in prison. The students were yelled at and "scared straight" so they could avoid prison life. After the film, many states introduced these types of programs to motivate these young people to change.

A 2000 study with Petrosino, Turpin-Petrosino, and Finckenauer found that these programs may be well-meaning but have harmful effects. Students who have participated in these programs have higher rates of re-arrest and delinquent behavior than those students who were not involved (Petrosino et al., 2000). There were many risk factors that led these young people to be incarcerated and put in Scared Straight. They may have been raised in a stressful home environment or subjected to abuse. Did being yelled at address any of those risk factors?

Another type of "fear-based" faulty prevention program are boot camps for young people. These camps isolate the teens from their peers and take away their connections from home and friends. There is an increasing amount of Internet or gaming boot camps. First originating in China, these "Internet addiction bootcamps" have caused controversy due to unscientific methods and unclear definitions of what exactly "Internet addiction" is. In China, electro-shock methods and beatings have happened in these camps. The *Washington Post* reported in 2017 that one teen that checked into one of these Chinese camps died two days after admission. The teen's body was covered in scars and bruises. That camp was shut down, but others advertising services in Internet and gaming addiction remain (Wang, 2017). And these camps are not just overseas.

Many residential treatment facilities or camps sell parents on the idea that their program can fix or cure problems with the Internet. For example, one facility called River View Christian Academy in California advertises that they remove "the distractions that often cause students to struggle" and ask on their front page, "Do they have a problem with internet addiction, social media addiction, pornography addiction or video game addiction?" (Rescue, 2020). None of these "addictions" are officially recognized by the DSM-V, the gold standard for therapists, psychiatrists, and psychologists for diagnosing mental health conditions.

These punitive programs are focused on the stick, not the carrot. The director of the Center for the Study and Prevention of Violence at the University of Colorado at Boulder, Del Elliot, said, "Many after-the-fact punitive reactions focus on deterrents rather than causes of the problem. Serious violence continues because the underlying problems are never addressed" (Elliott et al., 1998). These harsh punishments also erode trust and care in the parent-child relationship.

In addition to the harm that fear or punishment creates, removing adolescents from their peers and putting them with strangers their age can make problems worse. Phones are taken away; the teen is far from their caregivers and the structure of their school and family. They are thrust into an unfamiliar place with peers their age also dealing with issues. "Youth Violence: A Report of the Surgeon General" evaluated these boot camps. The 2001 report described "significant harmful effects on youths, with significant increase in recidivism. Youths are also placed with other delinquent youths, who are role models as they reinforce each other's desirable behavior" (U.S. Department of Health and Human Services, 2001).

Young people need role models; they need their parents and caregivers and friends. Instead they are given role models of camp leaders who yell or hit them, peers who are also struggling, or convicts who also yell. What kind of role models are these "experts" and participants in such prevention programs?

Another harm of these erroneous programs is the deterioration of trust between young people and adults. The U.S. Department of Health and Human Services National Institutes of Health also found these programs can have long-term, damaging effects (U.S. Department of Health and Human Services, 2001). When young people are yelled at or told exaggerated dangers, adolescents tend to dismiss and not believe the messages and discredit the messenger.

When older generations give hyperbole and scary stories, they contradict the experiences of those who are younger. This can make young people even more resistant to hearing from their elders.

As parents we may feel better when we lay down the law, yell, or share scary stories. But it's not effective. It's not addressing the WHYs of the behavior, plus it makes our children less likely to listen to us in the future.

D.A.R.E. and Scared Straight are two of the most well-known examples of bad prevention programs. But other programs and practices engage in the same tactics. How often do we share scary news articles on technology with our kids? Or do we flippantly say, "Get over it," or, "Just ignore it," when our kids encounter issues online? Neither practice is helpful, although it's simple and clear and may make US feel better.

Focus on the Cause, Not the Symptom

To truly become a digital parent, you need to understand the WHYs of your child's behavior: the cause, not the symptom. We blame the technology too much. Blaming the phone is like saying that people who have pneumonia use penicillin too much because you see them using penicillin a lot. You cannot see the microbes replicating in their body. Similarly, we cannot know what is in someone's mind when they make a decision online.

The causes of behavior are complicated and multi-faceted. Environment and genetics and just the day-to-day situations we find ourselves in influence our behavior. This book cannot address the very specific causes for your child's behavior. It doesn't know the genetic code of your child, all their experiences since birth, preexisting conditions, their friends and peers. Academics, experts, therapists, and educators do their best with generalities that work for a broad swath of people. This book will focus on general causes for certain behaviors.

For example, Table 2.1 simplifies some of those potential causes or risk factors.

This is certainly not an exhaustive list. There are many different risk factors for a behavior, each unique to an individual. This book will explore some of these behaviors in more detail in later chapters.

Looking at the chart, you can see how behaviors like shaming, yelling, boot camps, isolation, and punishment do not address the true causes and risk factors. They can even exacerbate the problem. If a child is using pornography and the parent punishes and shames

Table 2.1 Risk Factors for Digital Behaviors

Behavior	Risk Factor
Excessive gaming	ADHD, stress, anxiety, depression
Cyberbullying	Lack of sleep, lack of strong peer support, boredom, victim of cyberbullying
Pornography use	Lack of sex education or discussions on sexual behavior, victim of sexual abuse, peer pressure, boredom
Falling for an online scam	Lack of strong peer or family support, lack of digital literacy skills, desire to fit in

them, then they are even less likely to go to that parent with questions about sex. If a child uses games to deal with stress, and the parent takes them to a boot camp where they are outside and punished, they feel even more stressed.

This book will help you examine the WHYs and uses the prevention science framework. It's a framework that I, the author, have used with tens of thousands of students in my work—with data to support changes in knowledge, attitudes, and behavior. To become a digital parent, focus less on the digital and more on the parenting.

Summary Points: Prevention Science and Technology

- Prevention science is a multidisciplinary methodology that works to lessen or prevent dysfunctional human behavior.
- Prevention science is the framework used in this book to help parents and caregivers mitigate and/or prevent negative digital behaviors and attitudes.
- A risk factor is a potential cause of dysfunctional or delinquent behavior.
- A protective factor is something that can inhibit or stop the harmful behavior from occurring.
- Prevention programs that do not focus on the risk factors that can cause the behavior, or develop protective factors, are ineffective.

- Social emotional learning (SEL) skills are preventative factors. They include self-regulation, managing emotions, setting and achieving positive goals, and empathy. Research finds that they are effective in academic performance, lowering conduct problems and emotional distress, and reducing substance abuse.
- SEL skills are important for parents to develop to help mitigate and potentially prevent unhealthy digital behaviors and attitudes.
- The causes of behavior are complicated with many risk factors. Parents and caregivers should not assume technology is causing the problem.

References

DiPerna, James. Conversation with the author May 2020.

Elliott, D., B. Hamburg, and K. Williams. *Violence in American Schools: A New Perspective*. Cambridge: Cambridge University Press, 1998.

Ferguson, Christopher. Conversation with the author March 2020.

Lilienfeld, Scott O. "Why 'Just Say No' Doesn't Work." *Scientific American*, January 1, 2014. www.scientificamerican.com/article/why-just-say-no-doesnt-work/.

Petrosino, A.J., C. Turpin-Petrosino, and J.O. Finkenauer. "Well-Meaning Programs Can Have Harmful Effects: Lessons from the 'Scared Straight' Experiments." *Crime and Delinquency* 46, no. 3 (2000): 354–379.

Public Affairs. "Who Is at Risk." *StopBullying.gov*, December 4, 2019. www.stopbullying.gov/bullying/at-risk.

Rogers-Whitehead, Carrie. "What Prevention Science Tells Us about Cyberbullying." *ISTE*, June 19, 2018. www.iste.org/explore/Digital-citizenship/What-prevention-science-tells-us-about-cyberbullying.

Teen Rescue. "Teen Rescue: Texas Troubled Youth Boarding School." River View Christian Academy, June 2, 2020. www.teenrescue.com/.

U.S. Department of Health and Human Services. *Youth Violence: A Report of the Surgeon General*. Rockville, MD: U.S. Department of Health and Human Services, Centers for Disease Control and Prevention, National Center for Injury Prevention and Control: Substance Abuse and Mental Health Services Administration, Center for Mental Health Services; and National Institutes of Health, National Institute of Mental Health. Government Printing Office, 2001.

Wang, Amy. "A Teen Checked Into an Internet-Addiction Camp in China: He Was Dead Two Days Later." *The Washington Post*. WP Company, August 14, 2017. www.washingtonpost.com/news/worldviews/

wp/2017/08/14/a-teen-checked-into-an-internet-addiction-camp-in-china-he-was-dead-two-days-later/.

"What Is SEL?" *CASEL*. https://casel.org/what-is-sel/ (Accessed May 23, 2020).

Wilkins, N., B. Tsao, M. Hertz, R. Davis, and J. Klevens. "Connecting the Dots: An Overview of the Links Among Multiple Forms of Violence." *National Center for Injury Prevention and Control*, Centers for Disease Control and Prevention, 2014. https://www.cdc.gov/violenceprevention/pdf/connecting_the_dots-a.pdf.

Chapter 3

Generation Alpha
Parenting Around Tech in Young Children

A new generation is growing up—the Alphas. Children of Millennials are being born into a world different from that of their parents. This cohort, typically defined as being born in 2010 (although Pew Research puts that year at 2012), are being raised by the generation most likely to be on social media (Dimock, 2019). This generation will likely have their ultrasound pictures posted on Facebook, have a smart device listening to them in their crib, and be exposed to YouTube before they can speak.

Statistics show that the Alphas will be more likely to:

- *Have food allergies.* A 2018 paper out of the Mayo Clinic found that nut allergies in particular have tripled since the early 2000s (Economist, 2019).
- *Be raised by parents who are less religious and less likely to attend church* (Hotwire, 2020).
- *Be more diverse.* It is expected that 50% of children will be non-Hispanic white by 2020 (Hotwire, 2020).
- *Be only children.* Today about 18% of women have only one child, a rise from earlier generations (Carter, 2019).
- *Have older parents.* The median age when women become mothers has risen to age 26 from age 23 in 1994. Part of this is because of a drop in teen pregnancy rates, but also because increases in biomedical science have allowed older women to have children (Livingston, 2020).
- *Have increased rates of obesity.* UNICEF reported in 2019 that while malnourishment had dropped since the 1990s, 700 million children worldwide were either obese or undernourished (UNICEF, 2020).

- *Struggle with vision issues.* A 2015 study found that nearsightedness has doubled in the UK the last fifty years and optometrists are concerned about computer vision syndrome, caused by more screen time (WebMD, 2019).

This generation will reach adulthood in the 2030s in a world that is aging. They will bear the cost of that aging, when in the 2030s it's anticipated that humanity will reach its highest proportion of people over 60 ever (Wikipedia, 2020). This means a world that is geared towards a different population, in which tax and work burdens may be heavier. In addition to less government support, due to lower birthrates, these children may be taking care of their parents with less support from siblings and other family members.

Despite some negative global trends and changes, there are a lot of positive things to say about this growing group. A research study of over 3,000 Generation Alphas and adults in 2019 reported in Hotwire, a global communications agency, shares some hopeful statistics. The report says, "Generation Alpha brings with it a strong set of opinions about the world we live in today" (Hotwire, 2020).

Some of those strong opinions include:

- "Boys and girls should be treated fairly." Approximately 94% of Alphas say this, in contrast to just about two thirds of Boomer and Millennial men.
- "I want to be a Dad when I grow up." Alphas are growing up in homes where Dad is taking a larger role and is more involved than in previous generations.
- "I want to take care of the environment." This belief is higher among Alphas than their Millennial elders.
- "School safety is important." This generation has grown up in an environment of more school shootings; 97% of them say that "keeping children safe at school" is very important.

What do parents of Alphas think about technology? Screen time is an important issue, which will be explored more in Chapter 6. The Hotwire report finds that 68% of US parents think their children have too much screen time. Eighty-seven percent of these parents also think a lot about how technology will impact their children's careers (Hotwire, 2020). Parents are thinking a lot about technology and their young children. This chapter will help take that thinking to positive and proactive strategies for parenting around technology.

Developmental Stages

There is a lot of growing in these years. This chapter will focus on birth to age 8, when children start going through puberty. Understanding what your child's body and brain are going through can help you create family norms and rules around technology.

Newborn (0–2 Months)

During the sleep-deprived newborn stage, technology may be the least of your concerns. And that's okay. Your infant's needs are simple: touch, talk, diaper changes, and feedings. During these months they will start turning their head towards sounds and begin to smile and look at you. They will start making their own sounds closer to 2 months. From the day of their birth, newborns pay more attention to faces. Books with reds, blacks, and faces will interest your newborn more. If your child does not respond to sounds or watch things that move, that is a warning sign that you should talk to your pediatrician (Ages and Stages, 2019).

Technology advice for newborns:

- No screens for newborns. They need physical touch, eye contact, and your voice.
- Consider using a sound machine or an app that creates white noise to help soothe your newborn to sleep.

Infants (2 Months–1 Year)

Past the newborn stage, there is rapid growth and development. This is the time when critical parts of the brain are formed. Infants need security, safety, and touch. During this time of development your infant will start babbling. They will have their first recognizable word around 9 months. Your child will react more to your sound and noise more, and around 6 months will start responding to his or her name (CDC, 2020).

Infants start reaching for things around 4 months, rolling over at 6 months, and by 9 months they can sit up and will start trying to stand with support. Typically, infants start walking around 12–14 months. From infancy they will mimic your responses, watch activities, look for things, and start picking up objects around 6 months (CDC, 2020).

Infants are sponges and watch you carefully. They will also watch whatever media you put on. I remember holding my infant one evening while watching an action movie. I didn't think he was paying attention; he was kind of dozing, but then during a scene in which there were loud arguments, he started crying. He reacted to the noise and knew somehow that the words shouted on the screen were negative. Even background noise on screens can affect the responses and feelings of infants.

Technology advice for infants:

- Use limited technology such as FaceTime or other virtual calls.
- Try to limit background noise of televisions or other devices that talk. Your baby is learning sounds and words and the multiple conflicting sounds can inhibit that.
- Interactive apps with which you talk and use with your child can be appropriate. However, infants are teething and are learning through touch. They can chew on and touch a book, not a tablet.

Toddlers (1 Year–3 Years)

Toddlers are on the move and gaining independence. They want to learn and explore, talk and express themselves. Most brain development occurs during the first three years of life, so allow your child safe space for learning and provide lots of enriching activity and words. Read to your child regularly. Your toddler will also enjoy matching games, singing songs, coloring, and being active outside (CDC, 2020).

Toddlers learn names for things and start saying sentences. As you go through your day, identify the objects around you. Describe the process of tasks such as, "To get dressed, first we need to put on our underwear," and encourage them to follow simple instructions.

Your child will be moving around more. They can start walking alone, kicking a ball, running, climbing, throwing, and more at these ages. Encourage that movement in a safe environment. Store sharp objects and weapons out of reach, and monitor your child closely around water since drowning is the leading cause of death for toddlers.

Technology advice for toddlers:

- Your toddler is more mobile and has greater motor skills. They can use more interactive apps for which their touch is required. Consider puzzles or coloring apps for older toddlers. Other apps that identify names of objects can help them developmentally. More specific apps and resources will be described in a later chapter.
- The American Academy of Pediatrics recommends that toddlers age 2 and younger do not use screen media except for video chatting (Pediatrics, 2016).

Textbox 3.1

Research on infants and toddlers learning from 2D media has consistently found that they learn less compared to face-to-face interactions. This is called the "transfer deficit" (Barr, 2010). Research published in the *Journal of Experimental Psychology* has found this deficit also in interactive apps. Something a child learns from a TV show, an app, or software does not necessarily translate into real learning until that child is older (Moser et al., 2015).

There is also the "video deficit effect." Professor Rachel Barr describes this deficit in a journal article, stating, "Children learn less from television than they do from live demonstrations until they are at least 3 years old" (Barr, 2010).

While it is certainly better for parents to try to use educational and interactive apps for their young children than simply videos, they should not think that just because a child completed a puzzle on an app, they can do so in real life. Learning does not translate directly into practice for younger children. They need in-person instruction and communication.

Preschoolers (3 Years–5 Years)

There is a great degree of emotional development at these ages. Children notice the world around them more and show more empathy and concern for others. They can share a wide range of emotion and start labeling those feelings. Children at these ages can share and cooperate more and express their likes and dislikes. These feelings of independence mean that preschoolers will shove, hit, and yell to resolve conflict. Parents need to model and correct these behaviors, gently, as soon as they occur. Around age 4 or 5 they will start learning that these actions have negative consequences and can start empathizing when you tell them, "When you hit your brother it made him sad" (Alli, 2018).

They start around age 4 to begin to tell what's real and what's not real. Still, this new skill is being developed and parents should be cautioned not to share certain media with children who don't know if the monster in the show is real or not.

A preschooler's brain is full of activity and their neurological processing is twice as busy as that of a college student; they are receiving and processing mountains of data, which can affect them emotionally. Preschoolers need patience and kindness (CDC, 2019).

Technology advice for preschoolers:

- Preschoolers can understand more social rules and complex ideas. They also start understanding the concept of time around age 4. Implement and enforce technology rules at home. Keep them simple such as, "You can only see one *Sesame Street* show today." They are lacking impulse control and judgment, so keep those rules consistent and enforce them.
- Provide more social opportunities for children at these ages. Encourage group play, not solo activities online.
- There are more evidence-based technology tools at these ages. However, limit consumption to no more than an hour or two a day.
- Preschoolers need 10–13 hours of sleep a night. Make sure media use does not interfere with that and do not put TVs in children's bedrooms (CDC, 2019).

Young Children (5 Years–8 Years)

By the time a child is 6, their brain is about 90% of an adult size. Despite the size, there is a lot of organizing and changing until it is truly an adult brain, and that happens a lot in adolescence. Around age 7 their corpus callosum, the fibers connecting the two hemispheres of the brain, matures and children can better perceive the world in a concrete rather than a magical and egocentric way. Developmentally, children can better make longer-term plans and goals and forecast the future (CDC, 2020).

Children these ages focus less on themselves and notice more of what's around them. Friendships are more important. They express a desire to be liked, and a desire to express those likes. They can help out more at home, wait their turn, consider consequences of their actions, and help create rules at home.

Physically they continue to grow rapidly, although a bigger growth spurt happens later after puberty. They will become leaner and lose their baby teeth. They develop more muscle mass and can be more active in team sports. During these ages motor skills, particularly fine motor skills, continue to develop until puberty (CDC, 2019).

Technology advice for young children:

- Children these ages are better able to look forward into the future. Set goals together about their technology use.
- Around ages 7 and 8 children's friends are more of their world. This continues through puberty as the importance grows even more. Provide some online opportunities for them to talk with friends. Let them video chat or play a game online together.
- Young children need 9–12 hours of sleep a night. Do not put screens in the bedroom and don't let media impact their rest (CDC, 2019).

Technology Impacts on Language and Social Development

The early years of childhood are the prime times of language and social development. This is why the American Academy of Pediatrics (AAP) put out a recommendation in 2016 that parents limit screen time for children under two years of age. They also advise parents to limit technology until they reach school age (Pediatrics, 2016). This does not mean technology is inherently bad, but it is a barrier to communication and language, and between parent and child.

Michael Robb, Senior Researcher with Common Sense Media, describes the research on children aged 2 and younger. "From a developmental standpoint there are a lot of limitations on what very young children can learn. A lot of media that's produced is developmentally inappropriate." Robb goes on to describe research on *Baby Einstein* videos. These videos were produced in the late 1990s and in the early to mid-2000s were ubiquitous across households with infants. One study cited in the *New York Times* estimated about a third of all infants 0–2 years old had been exposed to *Baby Einstein* by 2002. But then the research started coming in. One study out of the University of Washington found that for every hour of infants watching videos, they knew six to eight fewer words than infants who watched no videos (Guernsey, 2007). Robb echoes this, saying, "Kids are not learning from that type of media" (Rogers-Whitehead, 2020, interview with Michael Robb).

When children get older the research shifts. Preschool-aged children can have more language benefits from media. "Decades of research with preschool-aged children have demonstrated that watching educational media at home is positively associated with preschooler's development of literacy," describes the text *Media and the Well-Being of Children and Adolescents* by Amy Jordan and Daniel Romer (2014). The authors particularly mention *Sesame Street* and *Reading Rainbow*, both US-government-funded shows on PBS. "Studies conducted immediately after *Sesame Street* began airing found that preschool-aged children who watched the most *Sesame Street*, learned the most." Other studies of *Sesame Street* with lower-income families found that children who watched the show at age 2 or 3 had a better vocabulary when they were 5 compared to children who did not watch *Sesame Street* (Jordan and Romer, 2014).

As children's brains grow, they learn differently. One constant, however, is the importance of parents and caregivers. "The AAP has softened their statement in 2016 to better reflect the reality of parents on the ground. The harm is more to do with the displacement for things that are more appropriate and enriching for children that age," said Robb. "What are things that are more appropriate for infants and toddlers." "It's a lot of serve and return language interactions with warm supportive reactions," said Robb. "Screens don't do well with replicating what's in the real world" (Rogers-Whitehead, 2020, interview with Michael Robb).

Some ideas for parents to support language development in young children include:

- Point out things on a tablet or screen when you see them.
- When shopping for groceries, point out what you're buying and the names for things.
- Put on songs in the car and sing together with your child.
- Provide shakers, bells, or other noise-making instruments to your child. Let them make noise during music time, and you can also use them when speaking to emphasize certain consonants and syllables.
- When reading to your child ask them, "What happens next?" and let them help tell the story. Read wordless picture books as

well as ones with language. Books with only pictures and no words allow you and the child to make the story together.

Another important way for parents to encourage language development is not letting the screen come between them and their child. Children need conversation, or as Robb puts it, "serve and return language interactions." Early learning can be stopped by a text, ping, notification, or something else coming from a screen. It is harder for young children to learn language when their conversations and interactions are continuously interrupted.

A 2015 study published in *Academic Pediatrics* studied the mobile device use of mothers and how that affected the interactions of their children. Over 200 mothers with children 6 years and younger were observed in the study. The researchers found no association with race/ethnicity, education, or parenting style and their mobile use. But they did find an association with mothers who used their devices having less verbal and nonverbal interactions with their children. The authors of the study say, "The importance of responsive face-to-face parent-child interactions in the development of language, cognition, and self-regulation abilities during early childhood is undisputed. These crucial daily interactions can be disrupted through family use of media. For example, adults utter fewer words, respond to fewer bids for attention and have lower-quality interactions with the children in their care when a television is on in the room with them" (Radesky et al., 2015). Parents are rightfully concerned about media use in their children. However, they should pay attention to their own consumption of media. They may be inadvertently affecting their child's language and social development more than any app can.

Tech Trends for Generation Alpha

What are the tech trends for Generation Alpha? This cohort of children, who likely had their ultrasound picture posted on Facebook, are in a different technological environment than the Gen Zs. Around the time when the first Alphas were born, in 2011, mobile phone ownership in the United States was at 35%, according to Pew Research (2019). In 2019, it grew into 81% of Americans owning smartphones. Social media use has also exploded. In 2005, when Pew Research first started tracking social media adoption by American adults, just 5% used a social media platform. In 2019, that was about three fourths of all American adults (Pew Research, 2019). The 2010s and the new generation of Alphas also brought new technology such as smart home devices, Chromebooks, and *Pokémon Go* and other augmented-reality games. Compared to Gen Z, the younger Alpha generation has grown up in an environment with more connected devices and social media.

YouTube

Karina Gathu is an educator and mother of a 3-year-old. As with many other children, YouTube is big in their home. "We basically use YouTube and YouTube Kids," she said. YouTube Kids, released in 2015, is a version of YouTube aimed at children 12 and younger. "YouTube Kids is great because it allows you to set a timer and doesn't have any ads," said Gathu. YouTube is everywhere and young children are on it. There are one billion hours of YouTube content watched each day, according to marketing agency Omnicore (2020) (Rogers-Whitehead, 2020, interview with Karina Gathu).

YouTube is the second-most-visited site in the world and an increasing number of people prefer video platforms rather than live television. One prediction says that by 2025, half of viewers under 32 will not subscribe to paid TV at all (Omnicore, 2020). YouTube's growth since being founded in 2005 has run concurrently with the rise of the youngest generation. Despite trying to primarily use YouTube Kids in her home, Gathu comments, "YouTube is less restricted than YouTube Kids, but also more of our default on TVs, which means we aren't usually setting a timer or anything." Now most TVs are smart TVs. Gathu describes that once her son "realized he could watch the same YouTube on a TV instead of our phone, it made it harder to regulate" (Rogers-Whitehead, 2020, interview with Karina Gathu).

The popularity of YouTube tracks with what my work with Digital Respons-Ability finds when surveying elementary students. Overall, YouTube is the most popular social media in this age group. While YouTube may not be seen as social media, its platform serves the same purpose and has similar functions: liking, sharing, following, and posting.

A spokesperson for YouTube quoted in the *Washington Post* said, "YouTube is not a site for people under 13" (Siegel, 2019). Yet reports from Common Sense Media said that there was only a very small group of youth that only used YouTube Kids (Siegel, 2019). With YouTube hardwired into TVs, like in Gathu's home, it is hard to avoid. Millennials started the process of rejecting cable and traditional TV; will Generation Alpha turn away from TV even more? The never-ending and constantly new YouTube poses different challenges related to self-regulation. The effects of YouTube will be described more in Chapter 8.

Apps Aimed at Children

Companies and marketers realize that Generation Alpha means money. Much of the research on Generation Alpha and more details about this cohort can be found on marketing websites, not educational ones. "Alphas are the surest path to their millennial parent's wallets," describes one 2019 *WIRED* article (Ellis, 2019). There are more apps, games, YouTube channels, and content directed at young children. Larger companies are following YouTube's example and making kid-friendly versions of their product. In 2020 Spotify launched Spotify Kids (Perez, 2020). Facebook Messenger has Messenger Kids. Alphas are growing up in a landscape of products and platforms catering to their interests.

There are laws and regulations around apps aimed at children as well as other software and websites. In September 2019 the US Federal Trade Commission (FTC) settled with YouTube for "violations of the Children's Online Privacy Protection Act (COPPA)" (Cohen, 2019). COPPA, passed by Congress in 1998, is a federal law that protects the privacy of children under 13. It requires commercial and online services directed at children to provide notices and get parent consent before any personal data is collected for kids under 13 (Nguyen, 2020).

The European Union (EU) does not have a separate law like COPPA that addresses children's online privacy. But there are provisions in the General Data Protection Regulation (GDPR) that ask operators to have a higher standard to protect children's data. While the GDPR has an age of consent where data can be collected, it can vary from country to country (Nguyen, 2020). In the US, states can decide to be stricter with implementing COPPA. California has done this, asking all commercial websites to include their privacy policies.

The landscape of children's apps, despite COPPA, can be fairly unregulated and difficult to navigate. The FTC reports that it's looking again at COPPA with the "rapid changes in technology" (Nguyen, 2020). It is hard to know from just a description what the app actually does. More information about children's apps will be discussed in Chapter 8.

Good Media for Generation Alpha

What should parents look for when examining the tech trends for the youngest generation? Michael Robb suggests parents use the three Cs when evaluating content. He said, "It's much more about the intersection of those three things that affect a child than overall amount of screen time" (Rogers-Whitehead, 2020, interview with Michael Robb).

First C: Child—Look at the individual child's interests and personality.

Second C: Content—What is the content of the media? Is it well made?

Third C: Context—What's the context in which the media would be consumed? Do children use it by themselves or with a friend or sibling? Is it media designed to be educational and/or used at school?

Context is particularly important at these ages. When I teach digital parenting classes I am asked a lot about filtering. Parents want to know ways to block or prevent their children from seeing certain content. For older children, tweens, and teens I do not recommend filtering. But for this age I do. Why? It's because of context. Young children don't have the background knowledge to understand what they are seeing. They are still engaged in "magical" thinking and navigating the world. For a young child who believes in the Tooth Fairy or Santa Claus, how could they distinguish properly between what's real and fake online? Young children also don't get the sarcasm and jokes seen online. They may not know that arguments or violence is acting or made up, and may be disturbed. The context is crucial in determining what's appropriate for children to consume online.

For an example of how the three Cs work, let's imagine a scenario for a fictitious child. Darren is 4 years old and loves his family pet, Oscar the dog. Darren gets scared of the dark and has nightmares sometimes and crawls into his parents' bed. He is also very energetic and loves to play outside. A popular TV show aimed at children's Darren's age is Nick Jr's *Paw Patrol* (Ashby, 2013). Using the three Cs, Darren's parents can evaluate if that's good for him in Table 3.1.

Selecting media for your children is not an exact science. Maybe season one would be better for your child but season two would not. Children's interests change as well. But it can be a guide to finding better content.

Programming for toddlers and preschoolers is full of gender stereotypes. A study put out by Common Sense Media which looked at over 150 articles, books, and other research found that

> gender stereotypes in movies and on TV shows are more than persistent; they're incredibly effective at teaching kids what the culture expects of boys and girls. What makes these messages stick—and harder for parents to counteract—is that they're timed for the precise moment in kids' development when they're most receptive to their influence.
>
> (Knorr, 2017)

Children ages 2–6 are learning about gender identity and noticing differences between girls and boys (Knorr, 2017). Parents and

Table 3.1 Using the Three Cs to Evaluate Media

Three Cs	Questions to Ask	Good for Darren?
Child	Will this show be too scary? Does it appeal to my child's interests?	Darren likes his pet dog and the show has dogs as main characters which would interest him. It's not too scary which is good since Darren can be frightened.
Content	What is the content of the show? What is the plot? Who are the main characters? Is the show representative of different genders and races?	The show has dogs that go on rescue missions. The main human characters are white and there are only two female main characters.
Context	Is this an educational show? Is it okay for home? When would my child be watching it?	*Paw Patrol* can be very commercial and there is a lot of merchandise attached to it. It's for entertainment, not education. Darren would watch it at home, not school.

Figure 3.1 *Paw Patrol* merchandise

caregivers want to make sure that they find good media with positive representation of groups and individuals. Consider finding some counter-stereotypes. For example, often the hero of preschool programming is a plucky and energetic boy who acts out aggressively. Find a show with a quieter boy who expresses his feelings. Better yet, find a show with a female hero.

Unfortunately, finding programming that has more gender equality is difficult. The term "Smurfette Principle" refers to the show *The Smurfs*, where all the characters are boys, except for one. This has been a consistent principle over two decades and on average there are two male characters for every female on TV and in movies (Campbell, 2017). This can be seen in the *Paw Patrol* example: there are six dogs that are the main characters, and only one is a girl. It can be difficult to find content that checks off all the boxes and answers the questions to the three Cs, but it's possible. More good media examples and resources will be shared in Chapter 8.

Creating Technology Norms at Home

Norms are all around us. It's why we say "bless you" when someone sneezes and say "hello" instead of "goodbye" when we answer the phone. They are unwritten rules that tell us what we value, how we act, and what's considered normal. Norms can be societal, global, or familial. All families have norms of what's expected and what's not allowed. These norms continually shift over time. As children are young, a norm may be bedtime stories each evening, but that will change as those children age and read independently.

We create norms around technology in our homes. Those norms are particularly important when children are young. When something is new we don't have any past expectations about it; we don't think, "We've always had it this way," because there was no past history. Before you got a cell phone you may have had an expectation not to be contacted unless it was an emergency. You may have made more phone calls because that was how you kept in touch with friends. You most likely had a home phone and there were certain norms and etiquettes on when and how you used that phone. But then technology changed and a cell phone changed all those norms. Now you text friends instead of call. You may have gotten rid of your home phone. And the expectation you aren't contacted on your cell phone except for emergencies may be gone.

Norms reflect our family values. If your family values meal times together, then a norm may be no technology at the table. If you are a family that likes to play video games together, you may create norms around how, when, and what you play. Norms are different for every family, and there isn't necessarily a "right" or "wrong" norm. What's more important is making sure your norms reflect your values. In addition, you want to be deliberate with the habits and rules you create at home. It's easier to create a habit than to break one. It's much harder to create new norms with teenagers than 5-year-olds.

Here are some examples of technology norms you may choose to adopt for your family. These are research-based norms that experts recommend. However, you must choose what is best and most realistic for your family.

- No devices at family meal times.
- No TV in the background with children 2 and younger.

- Mobile devices are not taken into beds.
- No TVs in bedrooms.
- Make sure everyone gets adequate rest and exercise and do not allow screens to interfere with that.
- Talk together about the content of media consumed.
- Review the content of media for young children.

One way to create norms is to have a family media plan. In the Appendix is a sample of questions to help you create your own family norms around media and devices.

When implementing norms at home we need to model them as parents and caregivers. Children are less likely to follow us, and teens may reject the rules completely, if we don't model the same behavior. That means if we ask for no devices at meal times, we also don't bring out our own devices.

It is hard to model good tech behavior. A big reason for the difficulty is that adults have to work. We have responsibilities and must respond to bosses and projects. We can't always disconnect at home as we would want to. To help overcome this difficulty, implement the strategy of narrative parenting.

Dr. danah boyd, author of *It's Complicated: The Social Lives of Networked Teens*, uses the term narrative parenting as a suggestion for parents to narrate what they are doing online (boyd, 2015). A young child may see a device as a plaything because their interactions with it involved an educational app or a YouTube video. When they see their parent look at their phone, they may think their parent is doing something fun without them. They may also see a parent using a device as ignoring them. Narrative parenting means that when we get a work text we say something like, "Mommy needs to answer this text from her boss real fast," instead of picking it up. It also involves teaching the child what a mobile device can do. "I'm finding out how to get to your aunt's," we can say as we use GPS.

The *Atlantic* piece "Dangers of Distracted Parenting" by Erika Christakis describes this effect of technology distracting parent-child interactions (2018):

> Occasional parental inattention is not catastrophic (and may even build resilience), but chronic distraction is another story. Smartphone use has been associated with a familiar sign of addiction: Distracted adults grow irritable when their phone use is interrupted; they not only miss emotional cues but

actually misread them. A tuned-out parent may be quicker to anger than an engaged one, assuming that a child is trying to be manipulative when, in reality, she just wants attention. Short, deliberate separations can of course be harmless, even healthy, for parent and child alike (especially as children get older and require more independence). But that sort of separation is different from the inattention that occurs when a parent is with a child but communicating through his or her nonengagement that the child is less valuable than an email. A mother telling kids to go out and play, a father saying he needs to concentrate on a chore for the next half hour—these are entirely reasonable responses to the competing demands of adult life. What's going on today, however, is the rise of unpredictable care, governed by the beeps and enticements of smartphones. We seem to have stumbled into the worst model of parenting imaginable—always present physically, thereby blocking children's autonomy, yet only fitfully present emotionally.

While narrating what we're doing on the device won't solve this problem, it can help older children understand their importance. However, with younger children who cannot grasp language and understanding the complexities of adult work, what we say isn't important, it's what we do. This means we do not only need device-free times for our families, but for us.

Conversation Starters for Children Ages 0–8

Here are some conversation starters for children these ages. For infants and toddlers who are still learning language, engage in questions. They may not understand everything you mean, but they want to hear your voice and get your attention. From the first day of their birth we need to continuously talk to our children.

- Show me how do you do that on (name of the device).
- What is your favorite thing to do on (name of the device)?
- What do you think will happen next in the (movie/show/game)?
- When I'm on my phone how does it make you feel?
- May I have your permission to share this (picture/video/quote) of yours?
- How did it make you feel when you saw that on (movie/show/game)?

Generation Alpha is experiencing a different childhood than their parents experienced. However, although the technology may be new, the needs of children remain the same. While you may be unfamiliar with the apps and influencers with which your children are engaged, you are familiar with your children. Parents are needed in these crucial growing years.

Summary Points: Generation Alpha

- Generation Alphas are born in 2010 or later. They are the children of Millennials.
- Alphas are more racially diverse and typically grow up in smaller families. They have more egalitarian opinions than previous generations and express strong feelings on school safety.
- Screens should be very limited at ages 2 and younger. Infants and toddlers learn from face-to-face interactions and live demonstrations, not videos and screens.
- At age 3, children can benefit from educational media as opposed to younger ages.
- Alphas have more connected devices in their home than previous generations, including smart devices like smart speakers.
- YouTube is the second-most-visited site in the world and much of its content is targeted to young children.
- To help determine good media for children, evaluate through the three Cs: child, content, and context.
- Families should start creating healthy technology norms and habits while their children are at a young age.
- Parents who are chronically distracted through phones and other technology can affect the language and social development of their children.

References

Alli, Renee A. "Emotional Development in Preschoolers: From Age 3 to 5." *WebMD*, October 22, 2018. www.webmd.com/parenting/preschooler-emotional-development#1.

Ashby, Emily. "Parent Reviews for PAW Patrol: Common Sense Media." *Common Sense Media*. Common Sense Media: Ratings, Reviews, and

Advice, August 8, 2013. www.commonsensemedia.org/tv-reviews/paw-patrol/user-reviews/adult.

Barr, R. "Transfer of Learning between 2D and 3D Sources during Infancy: Informing Theory and Practice." *Developmental Review: DR* 30, no. 2 (2010): 128–154. https://doi.org/10.1016/j.dr.2010.03.001.

boyd, danah. *It's Complicated: The Social Lives of Networked Teens.* New Haven: Yale University Press, 2015.

Campbell, Olivia. "Why Gender Stereotypes in Kids' Shows Are a Really Big Deal." *Kids TV Shows Gender Stereotypes.* Toxic Masculinity, December 5, 2017. www.refinery29.com/en-us/kids-shows-gender-roles-stereotypes.

Carter, Christine Michel. "The Complete Guide to Generation Alpha, the Children of Millennials." *Forbes,* February 25, 2019. www.forbes.com/sites/christinecarter/2016/12/21/the-complete-guide-to-generation-alpha-the-children-of-millennials/#5d8bd2362363.

"CDC's Developmental Milestones." *Centers for Disease Control and Prevention.* Centers for Disease Control and Prevention, December 5, 2019. www.cdc.gov/ncbddd/actearly/milestones/index.html.

Christakis, Erika. "The Dangers of Distracted Parenting." *The Atlantic.* Atlantic Media Company, June 16, 2018. www.theatlantic.com/magazine/archive/2018/07/the-dangers-of-distracted-parenting/561752/.

Cohen, Kristin. "YouTube Channel Owners: Is Your Content Directed to Children?" *Federal Trade Commission,* November 22, 2019. www.ftc.gov/news-events/blogs/business-blog/2019/11/youtube-channel-owners-your-content-directed-children.

"Computer Vision Syndrome: Causes, Symptoms and Treatments." *WebMD,* August 17, 2019. www.webmd.com/eye-health/computer-vision-syndrome#1.

"Demographics of Social Media Users and Adoption in the United States." *Pew Research Center.* Pew Research Center: Internet, Science & Tech, June 12, 2019. www.pewresearch.org/internet/fact-sheet/social-media/.

Dimock, Michael. "Defining Generations: Where Millennials End and Generation Z Begins." *Pew Research Center,* January 17, 2019. www.pewresearch.org/fact-tank/2019/01/17/where-millennials-end-and-generation-z-begins/.

"Early Brain Development and Health." *Centers for Disease Control and Prevention.* Centers for Disease Control and Prevention, March 5, 2020. www.cdc.gov/ncbddd/childdevelopment/early-brain-development.html.

Ellis, Emma Grey. "Marketers Wanted a New Generation to Target, Hence Alphas." *Wired.* Conde Nast, September, 17, 2019. www.wired.com/story/marketing-generation-alpha/.

Gathu, Karina. Conversation with the author April 2020.

"Generation Alpha." *Wikipedia.* Wikimedia Foundation, June 4, 2020. https://en.wikipedia.org/wiki/Generation_Alpha.

Guernsey, Lisa. "The Genius of 'Baby Einstein'." *The New York Times,* August 16, 2007. www.nytimes.com/2007/08/16/opinion/16guernsey.html.

"Home." *Ages and Stages,* May 30, 2019. https://agesandstages.com/.

Jordan, Amy B., and Daniel Romer. *Media and the Well-Being of Children and Adolescents*. New York: Oxford University Press, 2014, 176–177.

Knorr, Caroline. "Gender Stereotypes Are Messing with Your Kid." *Common Sense Media*. Common Sense Media: Ratings, Reviews, and Advice, June 19, 2017. www.commonsensemedia.org/blog/gender-stereotypes-are-messing-with-your-kid.

Livingston, Gretchen. "Childlessness Falls, Family Size Grows among Highly Educated Women." *Pew Research Center's Social & Demographic Trends Project*, May 30, 2020. www.pewsocialtrends.org/2015/05/07/childlessness-falls-family-size-grows-among-highly-educated-women/.

"Malnutrition in Children." May 19, 2020. https://data.unicef.org/topic/nutrition/malnutrition/ (Accessed June 4, 2020).

"Media and Young Minds." *Pediatrics* 138, no. 5 (2016). doi:10.1542/peds.2016-2591.

Moser, Alecia, Laura Zimmermann, Kelly Dickerson, Amanda Grenell, Rachel Barr, and Peter Gerhardstein. "They Can Interact, But Can They Learn? Toddlers' Transfer Learning from Touchscreens and Television." *Journal of Experimental Child Psychology* 137 (2015): 137–155. doi:10.1016/j.jecp.2015.04.002.

Nguyen, Tay. "GDPR Matchup: The Children's Online Privacy Protection Act." *International Association of Privacy Professionals*. GDPR Matchup: The Children's Online Privacy Protection Act, May 6, 2020. https://iapp.org/news/a/gdpr-matchup-the-childrens-online-privacy-protection-act/.

Perez, Sarah. "Family-Friendly Spotify Kids App Launches in the U.S., Canada and France." *TechCrunch*, March 31, 2020. https://techcrunch.com/2020/03/31/family-friendly-spotify-kids-app-launches-in-the-u-s-canada-and-france/.

"The Prevalence of Peanut Allergy Has Trebled in 15 Years." *The Economist*. The Economist Newspaper, October 19, 2019. www.economist.com/graphic-detail/2019/10/03/the-prevalence-of-peanut-allergy-has-trebled-in-15-years?cid1=cust/dailypicks1/n/bl/n/2019103n/owned/n/n/dailypicks1/n/n/NA/319028/n.

Radesky, J., A.L. Miller, K.L. Rosenblum, D. Appugliese, N. Kaciroti, and J.C. Lumeng. "Maternal Mobile Device Use during a Structured Parent-Child Interaction Task." *Academic Pediatrics* 15, no. 2 (2015): 238–244. https://doi.org/10.1016/j.acap.2014.10.001.

Robb, Michael. Conversation with the author March 2020.

Siegel, Rachel. "Tweens, Teens and Screens: The Average Time Kids Spend Watching Online Videos Has Doubled in 4 Years." *The Washington Post*. WP Company, October 29, 2019. www.washingtonpost.com/technology/2019/10/29/survey-average-time-young-people-spend-watching-videos-mostly-youtube-has-doubled-since/.

"Understanding Generation Alpha: The Most Diverse Generation Yet." *Hotwire*. www.hotwireglobal.com/feature/genalpha3 (Accessed April 1, 2020).

"YouTube by the Numbers: Stats, Demographics & Fun Facts." *Omnicore*, February 10, 2020. www.omnicoreagency.com/youtube-statistics/.

Chapter 4

The Tween Years
Puberty + Peers + Tech

Alice is 10 years old and the daughter of Ben Trentlemen. When interviewed, Ben excitedly talked about the new things his daughter would learn on YouTube. He was impressed by Alice's ability to seek and find videos related to her interest in art. Ben was not as excited to talk about an issue they had with Alice and YouTube.

"For Alice we noticed she was having a big issue with YouTube and she was really into the unboxing videos." Trentlemen described one series of videos in particular he calls the "Princess videos." "It was basically like this really rich girl that would play with her toys, and that would be it. And Alice definitely started to develop a problem with it. . . . [W]e found her in the room hiding with her iPod a few times."

Trentlemen said he understood his daughter knew she was spending too much time on the unboxing videos and knew her parents wouldn't approve. "We were all real and earnest about it," he said. "I had to sit down with her and have a conversation."

He asked Alice, "Does it feel good that you're hiding this from us? Do you feel you can control this?" Trentlemen goes on to say, "We came to the conclusion together that she wasn't ready to have YouTube on her iPod." Alice told her father that the "Princess" videos took her away from her own toys when she watched the girl in the video open her own toys. (Rogers-Whitehead, 2020, interview with Ben Trentlemen).

The ages of 8–13, the age Alice is right in the middle of, can be a fraught, fun, and frustrating time for both children and parents. Children these ages are bombarded by many influences: biological, cultural, peer, and technological. This chapter explores those influences and offers strategies of how parents can navigate these critical years as a child changes into a teenager.

Puberty

Children start going through puberty between 8 and 14, with girls typically starting earlier. Every child is different in how quickly or slowly and what stage they progress through puberty. This can be tough on young people who may feel they look different from their peers due to progressing at a different pace, but it's important to reassure your child that everybody is unique and this is very normal.

Some changes in puberty include:

- Increased sweating, possibly leading to body odors and acne
- Hair growth around genitals, on arms and legs, and under the armpits
- Development of breasts and widening of hips in females
- Bone growth and growth spurts
- Typically, menarche (starting of menstrual periods) in females
- Enlargement of the penis and testicles and deepening of voice in males
- More sexual thoughts and urges
- Stronger and more intense emotions with mood swings

(Planned Parenthood, 2020)

Puberty is governed by hormones which affect the person emotionally and biologically. It may lead to a tween feeling as though his life is out of control—and in some ways it is. The body releases a gonadotropin-releasing hormone which triggers additional hormones and spreads through the bloodstream. It's a cascade effect that affects the whole body.

That out-of-control feeling and hormones can make it appear that your child became a different person overnight. There's some truth to that feeling; puberty is typically triggered at night by the hypothalamus. Literally overnight, hormones can be released through the body and the child wakes up the next day feeling different (Planned Parenthood, 2020).

Textbox 4.1

One evidence-based online resource aimed at sex education for ages 10–14 is the site Amaze.org. It has age-appropriate videos and content for tweens going through puberty. This nonprofit has had its material viewed in almost 200 countries and was evaluated to find that its content helped encourage acceptance of diverse sexual orientation and gender identity and increased knowledge about sexual assault and consent (Amaze.org, 2020).

Puberty can be distressing to parents, but it's helpful to keep in mind that it's more distressing for the person going through it. A parent may have confused feelings, such as, "Where did my little boy go?" "Why is she acting that way?" But the child is also confused. During this time of transition and confusion it's important that a parent be a reliable and steady pillar to lean on. While it's understandable your feelings may also be shifting, it's best to set aside your own emotions and focus on your child. If your child feels he or she cannot confide and talk to you about their changes in their body, why would they come to you if they also experience troubles online?

Here are some statements to keep parents grounded during puberty:

- This is normal.
- Every child goes through puberty at their own pace.
- They will get through this; there is an end.
- I will be there for my child through ups and downs.
- I will keep consistent boundaries and affection.

Peer Influence

Along with the biological changes in puberty, there are big social changes. A parent who was once their child's "best friend" now is characterized as an enemy. Children get quieter and more secretive. A favorite pastime of parent and child is now put aside for time with friends. There is more eyerolling, backtalk, and defiance. While frustrating for parents, this is normal (Steinberg and Monahan, 2007).

During puberty a child's body changes to an adult's, which is capable of sexual reproduction. The body is pushing the child to get out of the home and eventually reproduce. They are leaving the nest, which means a rejection of caregivers and embrace of peers. A toddler's brain is similar; there is an instinctual drive to explore and take risks. But unlike a toddler brain, an older tween and teen brain has greater risks. The body also doesn't consider concerns like being in school with no job, or not having an adult brain; the body just wants to spread its genes. Physical maturation happens before emotional maturation in the prefrontal cortex. Humans finish their sexual development before the brain is fully developed.

According to the *Journal of Developmental Psychology*, the highest rate of peer influence is between ages 10 and 14—right during puberty (Steinberg and Monahan, 2007). These are the years when a child's friends become extremely important. These are the years when they listen to adults less. These are the years of mood swings and confusion. These are also the years of first phones and first social media accounts.

Textbox 4.2

In the book *Shame*, Stanford professor Mali Mann writes about the particular shames and feelings that come with puberty. She cites research by Mussen and Jones that "late-maturing boys were more likely than normally maturing boys to have feelings of personal inadequacy, feelings of rejection and domination by others, and prolonged dependency needs towards their parents." In general, boys who grow taller, get facial hair, and have their voices changed are admired by their peers. This is in contrast to girls. Mann writes, "Adolescent girls who mature early are at greater risk of depressive and anxiety symptoms than are girls who mature at the 'normal' time and get into more behavioral problems" (Mann, 2016).

Parents and caregivers should recognize this gender disparity that girls and boys are under different pressures. They should particularly monitor girls' feelings and moods (Shipman and Kay, 2018).

Your role and relationship with your child will shift as peers become more central to your child's life. You may find your child coming to you less with problems. They may be less affectionate with you in public. They both want your comfort and support, and independence. There's a push and pull.

This can hurt. You may feel rejected and unappreciated. To deal with those feelings of rejection, try to think back when you were their age. You probably had the same behaviors. You probably found your parents embarrassing. Recognize that your child is not being "mean" to you or deliberately trying to hurt you; they are growing and changing. This does not mean no rules or boundaries, but that you may need to enforce your values and rules differently than before.

Here are some suggestions to set boundaries and discipline tweens:

- *Be the mean parent.* This does not mean yelling, being rude, or name-calling. This means being willing to take on the role of scapegoat, or "mean parent" with your child. Developmentally, it is difficult for them to stand up to their friends. If they can blame you for tech rules and restrictions, it's easier than just saying "no." You don't care what their friends think about you. But they care what their friends think about them.

- *Do not discipline in public.* This relates to the first advice, being a mean parent. You need to let your child save face in front of their peers. This means not chastising them in front of their friends. It also means no disciplining online. Do not complain about your child in a post. And certainly do not ever record a video of you smashing their phone or shaming them online.

- *Stand firm and united.* If you and your partner decide on a rule, stand together on it. You must be united on topics of getting a phone, what apps they can use, etc. Your child may try to go between the two of you to get what they want.

- *Speak carefully about their friends.* Tweens want to protect their peer relationships. They do not want to "tattle" and may respond negatively if they feel you are judging their friends. Their friends are very important to them, so be careful what you say about those friends.

- *Don't put them on the spot.* Have a soft and gentle approach on delicate subjects. Instead of saying, "Why would you do that?" ask, "Why do you think your friend Javier did that?" or use an example from the news or media to bring up the topic. Share a story or a scenario to ease into the topic instead of directly blurting, "Why are you spending so much money on that game of yours?"

Tween Trends Online

What are tweens doing online? The answer to that changes rapidly. Children this age are always watching their peers and trying out new things. Apps and games gain popularity quickly, but also decline quickly.

For example, the online battle game *Fortnite* has risen and declined with spectacular speed. *Fortnite* is particularly popular among tweens: a Statistica survey in 2019 found that 45% of parents in the United States said their children had played the game (Gough, 2019). While exact statistics are hard to find, it appears the peak of number of players of *Fortnite* was in August 2018, coinciding with the release of Nintendo Switch and school being out. This is a very quick rise from being released in July 2017. *Fortnite* still remained popular in 2019, notably having an in-game concert in February of that year "attended" by over ten million people. But compared to 2018, *Fortnite* has declined in players, Twitch viewership, and revenue, having a 52% decrease from 2018 to 2019 (Cultured Vultures, 2020). *Fortnite* is still played by many children, and it and other games will be discussed in further detail in Chapter 7.

Keeping up with trends is difficult, and frankly, not the best use of a parent's time. Tweens have their own culture. They have their own languages, dress, customs, entertainment, and "gods" like specific influencers, actors, or other entertainers. A parent trying to fully understand tween culture is like a European explorer in the 1500s reaching a new village on an unexplored land. It is normal to not understand this culture; it's foreign. While parents should stay abreast of general trends, the specifics are less important. You are their parent, not their peer. You are not trying to fit into this culture. You will always be an outsider.

Caroline Knorr, Senior Parenting Editor with Common Sense Media, said, in "the tween and teen years, kids are looking for examples of what is cool in the world, how they should behave. They are starting to move into more of a peer-focused time of their lives" (Rogers-Whitehead, 2020, interview with Caroline Knorr). Tweens are observing the trends closely and know much sooner than any online think-piece what's "cool" and "not cool."

Children ages 8–13 use media differently than teens. From our surveys with Digital Respons-Ability we find that YouTube is consistently the most popular social media with this age group. While adults may not view YouTube as social media, the ability to follow, comment, and share puts it in that realm. YouTube is often the first exposure to media for children. Infants are given tablets or shown their parent's phone. Along with TV, it's the media that this age is more familiar with.

Textbox 4.3

From Digital Respons-Ability's surveys of tweens we find that the most popular social media is YouTube, followed by Instagram. While some tweens are on Snapchat at young ages like 8 or 9, the majority of tweens prefer different social media. Older teens are more likely to be on Snapchat, Facebook, and Twitter than tweens. With the growth of TikTok we have updated our surveys to track this newer and very popular social media platform.

According to the 2019 Common Sense Media census, 53% of tweens watch TV videos, but this drops to 39% when they hit their teen years. Tweens enjoy playing games like *Fortnite*, and the census reports that about a third of them are gamers. However, this number of self-identified gamers declines to about 22% as they become teens. These drops coincide with the first phone ownership. Mobile phone usage shapes media consumption. TV and gaming decline in the teen years, and social media use rises. A smaller percentage of tweens are on social media, about 4% in the census, but that grows to 16% when they hit 13 ("Media Use by Tweens and Teens 2019: Infographic: Common Sense Media," 2020).

The stats cited are generalized. It's important to remember that media consumption varies by race, gender, culture, and class. For example, the messaging app WhatsApp is over three times as popular with Hispanics than with white Americans. Pinterest is more popular with white women than with other groups and while popular with all races, Instagram has a particularly high following from Hispanic users (Perrin and Anderson, 2019).

The digital divide, or equitable access to high speed Internet and Internet-enabled devices, affects consumption. Pew Research finds that 15% of households with school-age children do not have high-speed Internet connections at home. This number jumps to 35% for families that make less than $30,000 a year and the gaps are "particularly pronounced in black and Hispanic households with school-age children" (Auxier and Anderson, 2020). These households are also less likely to have access to a home computer. They may be completing their homework and doing much of their interactions on a mobile device.

Every tween is an individual and has his or her own patterns and platforms of media consumption. But in general, as of this writing tweens enjoy playing video games and watching YouTube and TV, and are less likely to have a mobile phone or be on social media.

Developmentally, what kind of media should tweens consume? Knorr speaks about the importance of role models. Tweens are looking to peers and others to navigate the world. "So, around that age we look at media that is very pro social, and that moves into positive role models," she said. These positive role models should reiterate the values and norms in the home. They should be representative; tweens should see characters that look like them. Knorr recommends media "where people make a mistake and learn from that mistake" (Rogers-Whitehead, 2020, interview with Caroline Knorr).

Pro-social role models can come from many different platforms. It can be the gamer friend who encourages the tween to try again when they fail. It can be an influencer who speaks authentically about the work it took to gain followers. A TV show with diverse characters who argue but still remain friends can be that positive influence. Parents can and should be that positive role model. Even if they are explorers of this foreign culture and may feel out of their depth, they can be an example and model pro-social behaviors.

First Phones and Social Media Accounts

When I talk to parents and teach classes I inevitably get this question: "What's the best age to get a child their first smartphone?" That's a question that's difficult to answer because it depends on the child and family. There are good reasons to have a phone at younger ages. Perhaps the child lives in multiple households, or is involved in many afterschool activities. A tween may be responsible for watching younger siblings. I don't have a firm answer to this question but I ask parents to ask themselves and their child this question and consider where their child is developmentally.

The tween years are when children typically get their first phone. According to a Common Sense Media report in October 2019, at age 8 only 20% of children own a smartphone ("Media Use by Tweens and Teens 2019: Infographic: Common Sense Media," 2020). Eight-year-olds with phones are a minority. However, 13-year-olds without phones are a minority. From ages 8 to 13 that number of smartphone owners increases until about three quarters of 13-year-olds have their own phone. This means your 8- or 9-year-old is probably not asking for a phone; maybe only three or four students in their class have one. But your 13-year-old will most likely be clamoring for one ("Media Use by Tweens and Teens 2019: Infographic: Common Sense Media," 2020). When they look around their classes it will appear that everyone has one, and that's close to true.

If your family has decided to hold back on phones during these years, that's okay. However, consider some smartphone alternatives. Smartphones are not just communication devices, they become more essential for coordination and pick-up as children branch out into extracurricular activities and independence. Consider purchasing your child a smartwatch that can make calls and has GPS, or a "dumb" phone which only makes calls. Another option is to strip down and disable Internet on an older model smartphone. There are options between no phone at all and an Internet-enabled smartphone with all the apps. For more information about creating a family media plan, see the Appendix.

Textbox 4.4

There are many Internet-enabled devices besides phones. One time, teaching a digital parenting class, I got a question from a mother about how her son was able to bypass their rules around no Internet. He didn't have a phone or tablet, but he did have a Nintendo DS. Handheld gaming systems can connect to the Internet. As more games shift to a subscription or access code model, the Internet is essential to play them.

If you have family rules about limiting Internet access to your teen, or want that access to have filters, be aware that children can access the Internet other ways. These Internet of Things (IoT) items can also be a way for your child to get online.

- *STEM toys*. In particular, robots you can code like Dash, Dot, and LEGO Mindstorm require and use the Internet.
- *Fitness trackers*. Some children's fitness devices such as Garmin's Vivofit and Leapband can connect and update online.
- *Walkie talkies*. Some can connect to WiFi while others just use radio waves.
- *Stuffed animals with Bluetooth*. CloudPets, a company that made such animals with microphones, had several hacking scandals and went out of business.

These toys are also a cybersecurity risk. The Federal Trade Commission recommends that parents check any smart toys before giving them to their children. They recommend parents examine if the toys have a camera or microphone, what data is collected, and more (Miranda, 2019). Manufacturers in the United States are required to disclose their privacy practices and get consent before collecting data from children.

Before giving your child their first phone, discuss these questions:

- What are tech-free times?
- What are tech-free areas of the home?
- Who is responsible for charging the phone?
- What time does the phone get put away at night?
- Who repairs and pays for the phone if it's damaged or lost?
- What information must be shared with parents?
- What are the passwords to the device?
- Who purchases apps/games for the phone?
- Will this phone be shared with younger siblings or others?

At these younger ages parents should know passwords and help manage their children's devices. This means approving downloads, knowing how to get into the phone and any social media accounts, being able to find the phone through GPS, and having access to the phone when they ask. Be clear that this is a phone that you as a parent or caregiver are giving to them because they need it and you trust them. The phone is a privilege and as the parent who pays for the apps, phone, and Internet, you should have access to the phone.

Inevitably with the first phone comes the first social media accounts. If a tween has not created an account before their first phone, they probably will then. Thus, there needs to be two discussions between you and your child: responsibilities of owning a phone, and creating the first social media accounts.

When surveying students this age, I have found many who have social media accounts before the age requirement. The most popular social media apps like Facebook, Instagram, Snapchat, and TikTok all recommend their apps for ages 12 and older. However, many students do not wait that long. I recommend to parents having the conversation before age 12 about social media and if a child has a strong desire to get an account, consider creating an account with them.

By creating a social media account with your tween together, this gives you an opportunity to talk about settings, talk about public and private information, create the profile together, and more. Caroline Knorr echoes this advice. "We believe that something like Instagram is OK if you can manage it and monitor it and you're aware that your kid is getting tracked." Her work with Common Sense Media has also found that "a lot of kids register it under an older age. We're aware of that so we try to factor in reality" (Rogers-Whitehead, 2020, interview with Caroline Knorr).

Every child is different. Some may express no interest in social media, and that interest can vary by gender and culture. Typically, girls use social media more, and report liking at higher rates than boys their age. African-American and Hispanic teens enjoy social media more than whites. A 2018 study out of Pew Research found that eight out of ten African-Americans find social media to be a tool for political advocacy (Pew Research, 2018). White Americans, in contrast to those of color, think social media platforms have a negative impact. Talk to your child to gauge their interest.

If you decide to create a social media profile with your child, here are some items to consider:

- *Examine the settings.* Social media apps default on public settings, not private. For example, Instagram has a default private setting which only allows followers you approve to see what you share. Keep in mind that people can still share photos and videos directly over Instagram even if they're not following you. This is the same case with Facebook, which allows messages from non-friends, although those messages go to an "Other" inbox.
- *Look at inboxes.* On some apps parents can disable the chatting feature. For example, *Roblox*, a popular social building game for this age group, has a chat function. Some social media does not allow you to completely disable the chat function, like Facebook Messenger. If parents want control over messages in Facebook, they need to use Messenger Kids (Perez, 2020).
- *Restrict purchasing functions.* Social media is not just for communication, it's become a location for sending money and making purchases. Instagram offers Instagram Checkout with which people can make purchases directly through the app (Instagram Help Center, 2020). *Roblox* offers Robux, which allows you to get in-game upgrades. Facebook allows peer-to-peer payments through Messenger. Parents should make sure that no credit

Table 4.1 Public and Private Information on Social Media

Public Information	Private Information
Name	Location
Public profile picture	Other pictures
Username	Friends and contacts
Bio (although some social media does not require this)	Interests, hobbies, saved links, and videos

card is attached to the phone and that purchases are restricted or blocked.

- *Discuss what's private and public.* Discuss with your child what to share and what NOT to share online. You cannot always decide what information you want to share on a profile. For example, in Snapchat, a name, birthdate, email, and cell number are required. When creating profiles, try to leave out personal information like location. Understand that if you're using multiple social media profiles, you lose some of that privacy. For example, if you post on Facebook from Instagram, more people can see that post. Table 4.1 summarizes what parents should communicate to tweens about what is private and what is public information online.

- *Share moderation tools.* Empower your children to take control over the feed. If they are unhappy with a follower or things they see online, they have a degree of control. Teach them to hide posts, block followers and/or friends, and report content to the social media platform.

For more specific information about apps and social media, see Chapter 8.

Setting Boundaries

Technology makes it hard to set boundaries. Constant messages, notifications, and content requires a high degree of self-regulation, a skill that children are still developing. Parents must help their children set these boundaries, and recognize that it is harder for children to step away from technology than it was when they were kids.

The growth of processing speeds and computer memory has made digital entertainment not a pastime, but an all-time hobby. When you were young you may have had the Internet, but it was slow and there was far, far less content. You may have also had a console, perhaps a Nintendo or Sega Genesis, or if you're older, an Atari. Those games were radically different. Compare the original *Legend of Zelda* game that was released in 1986 to the 2017 release of *The Legend of Zelda: Breath of the Wild* on the Nintendo Switch (Wikipedia, 2020). The Switch game is 13.4 gigabytes, compared to the original *Zelda* which only had 8 bits. This means there is roughly 107 billion times more memory in the 2017 game (Hussain, 2017). While *The Legend of Zelda: Breath of the Wild* is a large game, it's still not the largest on the market. By backing up memory on the cloud, those games can be three times as large.

I played the original *Legend of Zelda* as a child, and beat it in a day. I also played *The Legend of Zelda: Breath of the Wild* with my family, and it took about four months of playing off and on to beat it. You could also argue you can never truly beat *Breath of the Wild*, because since we beat that game in Spring 2018 my son still plays it occasionally years later, finding new treasures and secrets.

Games don't have endings like they used to. World-building games like *World of Warcraft* never end. Thus parents need to adjust their expectations and not ask, "Are you done with that game yet?" Setting boundaries and limits with never-ending entertainment is vital for children to succeed at school and, as they age, in the workplace. Someone who cannot put away a device or game to go to bed on time, or finish their project, or see a friend, may suffer not only financially but emotionally.

Ben Trentlemen describes setting boundaries with his two children:

> We do try to help out the kids with boundaries and recognize those things. It is interesting to see with the unlimited access of things, like watching a TV on Netflix, there's so much variety available. Left up to their devices they could watch the same show 6 hours straight. They are entranced by this thing that can continually fuel them. They love to watch Vines on YouTube—it's the same thing, it's this unending thing that doesn't have any structure of a narrative story. There's not a beginning, middle or an end. It's basically watching a continuous climax of a story. It's always the peak of the interest of this thing, there's not really any come down from that.
>
> (Rogers-Whitehead, 2020, interview with Ben Trentlemen)

Trentlemen raises an important point. Not only do games and entertainment never end, but there's something around the corner.

There's always a next boss or quest. There's a constant climax and level of excitement. A Vine video is only six seconds long, so it's just one six-second climax of a story. It is particularly difficult to stop a story at its climax.

Ben mentions how he has "to be deliberate" with entertainment for his 10- and 7–year-old. He puts on a movie instead of a TV show. A TV show has episode after episode, but a movie has a beginning, middle, and end. "I know if there's a movie it comes to an end," Ben said. "Their energy level follows the ebbs and flows as it comes to a conclusion" (Rogers-Whitehead, 2020, interview with Ben Trentlemen).

Parents need to be strategic and deliberate when setting boundaries around media. Here are some suggestions for parents:

- *Don't allow unlimited use of a device.* "We don't give the kids unlimited use of the thing," Trentlemen said. "We don't store them in their rooms; they're always in my room or plugged in a communal space." This rule should also be applied for parents.
- *Fewer videos and more movies.* YouTube and its algorithm that constantly recommends the next video is harder for children to step away from. Watch a movie together as a family: not only does a movie have a clear beginning and end, it's a communal way to have conversations about media.
- *Set limits on gaming.* For games that never end or are more of a sandbox style, have limits on play and bedtime. For example, the child can play 30 minutes of *Minecraft* a day, but no more unless it's arranged in advance. For more gaming advice, see Chapter 7.
- *Adjust settings on devices.* Use timers on phones and apps. Have phones and tablets automatically go to night mode at a certain time of day, or shut off completely. YouTube Kids has a built-in timer that shuts down the app after a certain prescribed time. You can also use an old-fashioned alarm clock or set a timer on a smart home device. More strategies on screen time will be discussed in Chapter 6.

As children age and their brains develop, self-regulation becomes easier. The portion of the brain tasked with long-term planning is the prefrontal cortex, which develops last. This means setting limits is biologically hard for children, and parents need to help with those boundaries.

Conversation Starters for Children Ages 8–13

It can be difficult for parents to talk about technology. But they must, particularly at these ages when so many changes are happening and they are starting to get online independently (Rogers-Whitehead, 2020).

Here are some conversation starters for children these ages. Remember to use open-ended questions such as those that start with What, Why, and How instead of Do or When.

- What things are private to you? What things are public?
- Will you be able to finish your homework on time to (play game/watch show)?
- Who are your friends online?
- Do those friends ever do things that make you uncomfortable? What do you do when you feel uncomfortable?
- What are some things you like to do online with me and the rest of your family? What is something we do that you don't like?
- How do you feel about how much time I spend online? How can I improve?
- How would you feel if someone shared something private about you online without your permission? Have I ever done that?

These ages of development are both fraught and fun. Children are rapidly changing into teens and discovering who they are. Technology also becomes a bigger part of their lives, as well as friendships. Parents must be involved to help guide and advise them through these critical years.

Summary Points: The Tween Years

- Children experience puberty typically between the ages of 8 and 14. This time brings both biological and emotional change.
- Tweens are highly influenced by their peers, a developmentally appropriate milestone that can affect technology use in the home.
- The desire to fit in with peers means tweens will try out many new types of technology and watch tech trends closely.

- Find pro-social role models for tweens online. They are looking to peers and influencers to figure out how to navigate the world.
- Children usually get smartphones around these ages. By age 13 about 75% of teens have smartphones, while only about 20% of 8-year-olds have them.
- Create social media accounts with your tween, adjust settings, and have conversations on what is public versus private information.
- Set boundaries at home on device usage and game play.

References

"Age Appropriate Info on Puberty for Tweens and Their Parents." *Amaze.* https://amaze.org/ (Accessed April 3, 2020).

Auxier, Brooke, and Monica Anderson. "As Schools Close Due to the Coronavirus, Some U.S. Students Face a Digital 'Homework Gap'." *Pew Research Center*, March 16, 2020. www.pewresearch.org/fact-tank/2020/03/16/as-schools-close-due-to-the-coronavirus-some-u-s-students-face-a-digital-homework-gap/.

"Eight-in-Ten Blacks Say Social Media Help Shed Light on Rarely Discussed Issues: The Same Share of Whites Say These Sites Distract from More Important Issues." *Pew Research Center*. Pew Research Center: Internet, Science & Tech, July 10, 2018. www.pewresearch.org/internet/2018/07/11/public-attitudes-toward-political-engagement-on-social-media/pi_2018-07-10_social-activism_0-20/.

Gaming, and 2020 Cultured Vultures. "How Many People Play Fortnite in 2020?" *Cultured Vultures*, May 23, 2020. https://culturedvultures.com/how-many-people-still-play-fortnite/.

Gough, Christina. "Fortnite Popularity among Children in the U.S. 2018." *Statista*, December 3, 2019. www.statista.com/statistics/985792/fortnite-playing-children-united-states/.

Hussain, Tamoor. "Nintendo Switch Digital Game File Sizes Revealed." *GameSpot*, February 20, 2017. www.gamespot.com/articles/nintendo-switch-digital-game-file-sizes-revealed/1100-6448026/.

"Instagram Help Center." Controlling Your Visibility | Instagram Help Center. https://help.instagram.com/116024195217477/ (Accessed March 25, 2020).

Knorr, Caroline. Conversation with the author March 2020.

"The Legend of Zelda." *Wikipedia*. Wikimedia Foundation, June 5, 2020. https://en.wikipedia.org/wiki/The_Legend_of_Zelda.

Mann, Mali. "Puberty, Adolescence, and Shame." In *Shame*. London: Routledge, 2016. https://doi.org/10.4324/9780429480089.

"Media Use by Tweens and Teens 2019: Infographic: Common Sense Media." Common Sense Media: Ratings, Reviews, and Advice. www.commonsensemedia.org/Media-use-by-tweens-and-teens-2019-infographic (Accessed March 17, 2020).

Miranda, Cristina. "What to Ask before Buying Internet-Connected Toys." *Consumer Information*, December 9, 2019. www.consumer.ftc.gov/blog/2019/12/what-ask-buying-internet-connected-toys.

Perez, Sarah. "Messenger Kids Adds Expanded Parental Controls, Details How Much Kids' Data Facebook Collects." *TechCrunch*, February 4, 2020. https://techcrunch.com/2020/02/04/messenger-kids-adds-expanded-parental-controls-details-how-much-kids-data-facebook-collects/.

Perrin, Andrew, and Monica Anderson. "Share of U.S. Adults Using Social Media, Including Facebook, Is Mostly Unchanged since 2018." *Pew Research Center*, April 10, 2019. www.pewresearch.org/fact-tank/2019/04/10/share-of-u-s-adults-using-social-media-including-facebook-is-mostly-unchanged-since-2018/.

Planned Parenthood. "Puberty in Females and Males: Get Facts and Info about Puberty." *Planned Parenthood*. www.plannedparenthood.org/learn/teens/puberty (Accessed March 8, 2020).

Rogers-Whitehead, Carrie. "Educators: Help Parents Talk to Their Kids about Tech." *ISTE*, February 25, 2020. www.iste.org/explore/educators-help-parents-talk-their-kids-about-tech.

Shipman, Claire, and Katty Kay. "How Puberty Kills Girls' Confidence." *The Atlantic*. Atlantic Media Company, September 21, 2018. www.theatlantic.com/family/archive/2018/09/puberty-girls-confidence/563804/.

Steinberg, L., and K.C. Monahan. "Age Differences in Resistance to Peer Influence." *Developmental Psychology* 43, no. 6 (2007): 1531–1543.

Trentlemen, Ben. Conversation with the author January 2020.

Chapter 5

Digital Identities
Teens and Technology

Who are you online? Who do you want to be online? Those are questions we ask teens with Digital Respons-Ability when teaching digital citizenship. Those are questions the teens may not know an answer to. But during these years before adulthood they are working on finding it out. Teens are developing both their real-life and digital identities. They are going through this process with an onslaught of information, hormones, expectations, and questions. Sometimes their digital identities are the same as in real life, sometimes they are different. Sometimes they have multiple identities, trying on new faces and new ideas. This can be a stressful process not just for the teen, but the parent.

Jess Stahle is a parent of a 10-, 13-, and 16-year-old and is in charge of parent programming at her local LGBTQ+ organization. She describes this identity forming with her child:

> I've noticed that my 13-year-old more and more. They are building more than just their digital identity, but a lot of their all-around identity based around opinions that they read online and adopting them as their own. So, if a bunch of sites are like "oh no this movie is terrible for these reasons" without seeing the movie my child is adopting those views. . . . There's this culture of trolling that I see them starting to reflect so we have a lot of conversations. Because there is a lot of blurring of lines between the digital self and the IRL self, especially with the younger kids. We discuss the difference between silly and joking and trolling and bullying, because I definitely see that blurring of that line.
> (Rogers-Whitehead, 2020, interview with Jess Stahle)

Identify forming can be both positive and negative. That process of figuring out who you are as a tween and a teen includes peers.

Having strong positive peer role models is a protective factor but having peers that encourage negative behaviors is a risk factor. Stahle has seen the influence of peers in her work with LGBTQ+ teens. She's found that these teens have developed their own online groups to support each other on Instagram or Facebook Messenger. "When hard things happen, at least in the experiences I've witnessed, that is where teens are turning with some really intense issues to get some support from each other . . . it's like the positive side of call out culture" (Rogers-Whitehead, 2020, interview with Jess Stahle).

While parents may feel left out or bewildered by their teen and the pace of technology, they still perform a very important role along with their child's friends. Christopher Ferguson, a professor of psychology who researches media, reminds parents of their part in the process and cautions them that kids grow up:

> There is a place for a responsible, non-fear-based training for kids to manage technology. It is a training process. Sometimes kids may be prone to releasing more personal information than they should. Or they may be prone to making fights on Instagram and saying things they shouldn't always say. Or sometimes it's just basic time management and that they need to do homework and get adequate sleep. It's just teaching them the habits. They're not going to be perfect and it may not go 100% like you want to. . . . If they get a job they can buy their own cell phone and you can't do anything to shut them down. We pay for the stuff right? So, we can shut stuff down? That's not going to be an option once our kids hit the adult years.
> (Rogers-Whitehead, 2020, interview with Chris Ferguson)

The trainings are different for teens than for younger ages. Parents need to take a step back and have fewer restrictions. Parents also need to shift from a parental to a mentorship role. Instead of closed-ended questions like, "Did you do your homework last night?" parents can engage more in motivational interviewing, asking, "What are ways that we could make it easier for you to complete your homework in the evening?" At these ages there should also be more conversations about healthy relationships, consent, and gender and sexuality. Technology should be viewed less as an obstacle or bogeyman, but as a tool for teens to find a job, attend college, and express their identity. It is not just teens that are navigating and shifting identities; parents are too. This chapter will share strategies and research to help you and your teen pilot through digital minefields and opportunities.

Teen Development

"Adolescence is one of the most fascinating and complex transitions in the life span. Its breathtaking pace of growth and change is second only to that of infancy," cites the text *Adolescent Development and the Biology of Puberty* (ADBP, 1999). The process of puberty begins around 8 or 9 years old and typically completes around ages 13 and 14, although this can vary with the teen. Girls typically start menstruation around ages 12 or 13 after their breasts develop (Shroff, 2018). Boys typically start and end puberty later, some continuing growth up to age 21. Although the most dramatic changes of puberty like periods, voice changes, pubic hair, hormonal changes, and more are complete around age 14, the teen body continues to grow. Girls typically reach their full height between ages 17 and 19 and boys grow more facial hair as they age (Morin, 2019).

The body is doing a lot of heavy lifting in adolescence to prepare the individual for the next stage of development:

> Research conducted with both humans and nonhuman primates suggests that adolescence is a time for carrying out crucial development tasks: becoming physically and sexually mature, acquiring skills needed to carry out adult roles, gaining increased autonomy from parents, and realigning social ties with members of both the same and opposite gender.
>
> (ADBP, 1999)

Other physical changes for teenagers include:

- Eating more
- Stronger sexual desires
- Ability to communicate like adults
- Gaining more muscle, particularly with boys
- Voices continue to deepen in boys
- More acne in both genders
- Hormonal mood swings, starting to lessen around age 15

Brains also continue to develop at these ages. The last part of the brain to develop is the prefrontal cortex, responsible for long-term planning and decision-making. This means a teen may be sexually mature before they are cognitively mature (Morin, 2019).

Textbox 5.1

Around puberty, adolescents have an adjustment in their body clocks. This is a natural shift that pushes their awake hours until later in the day. At bedtime a teen's body will stay up hours longer, and they can struggle to wake up in the morning. Unfortunately for teens, their school schedule and the wider world is built for early risers. Research shows that the effects of lack of sleep are strong and wide ranging. Not having enough sleep can increase anxiety, depression, irritability, and aggression, is attributed to weight gain, and can affect learning.

Technology exacerbates the shift in body clocks for teens. Staying up late on devices can interrupt a healthy bedtime. In addition, the blue light produced by those devices sends a message to the body to stay up. By rising later, teens have limited exposure to the morning light, or blue light, which tells the body to wake up.

Teens are not lazy by wanting to sleep more. Their bodies at this age need more sleep than an adult. More information about bedtime and sleep will be explored in Chapter 6.

Sexual Development

Shafia Zaloom, sexual educator and author of the book *Sex, Teens and Everything in Between: The New and Necessary Conversations Teenagers Need to Have About Consent, Sexual Harassment, Healthy Relationships and More*, wants people to know that "sex is a healthy, normal part of life" (Zaloom, 2019). The idea that their teen, who in the perspective of parents just used to be young child, may want to have or be having sex may be difficult. Parents may struggle with adjusting that their child is fast approaching adulthood, and thus engaging in adult activities.

Zaloom emphasizes that sexual desire is normal in the teen years. "Adolescence is a time of discovery," but she cautions,

> Yet not all teens are, or should be, experimenting with sexual relationships. . . . But every high school student—whether they're engaging in sexual activity or not—is exposed to all of these issues through their friends, the media, and the online

world every day. As parents we have to break the silence and
talk with our teens about healthy relationships and sexual consent, without shame, guilt or judgment. It's a matter of protecting our kids from and preventing harm.

(Zaloom, 2019)

A person reaches sexual maturity in his or her teens. That means
they are capable, just like adults, of having sex and carrying children. There is a gap between the social and emotional and physical
in teens. Parts of their bodies are developed, while others are growing. This makes parenting harder to discipline and set boundaries
in these proto-adults. But it's important that adults are part of this
process.

Sex and the Digital World

There is sex throughout our online world. Our children will be
exposed to it, and more. A meta-analysis published in 2018 in the
Journal of Adolescent Health estimated that about 20% of adolescents aged 12–16.5 will experience unwanted sexual exposure,
and 11.5% will experience online solicitation (Madigan et al.,
2018). Unwanted solicitations refer to requests to engage in sex
talk, share pictures, view pictures, or share personal sexual information. The unwanted exposure may come in the form of pop-
ups, spam, or exposure through a friend's or family member's
devices.

These experiences and exposures are sharing plastic and vulnerable brains. Sex educator Shafia Zaloom said,

Teen brain development is a process that goes on into the early
to mid-twenties . . . experience shapes the neuroplastic teen brain
and establishes patterns of behavior. Therefore, it is essential that
we talk to teenagers about the images of sex they see every day
and provide opportunities to identify and make sense of what
behaviors are illegal and criminal as well as legal and ethical.

(Zaloom, 2019)

That's an important point to make: there is the law and there are
ethics. Some sexual content may not be illegal, but unethical. And
there are harms beyond nudity in sexual content such as misogyny,
stereotypes, lack of consent, racism, and misinformation about sex.

It's important to keep in mind not to exaggerate harms and consider the young person's perspective. Some teens may not find sexual content offensive or a problem. If a parent focuses solely on sexual content and the child does not see it the same way, that child may be less likely to listen to their parent. In a 2011 survey from EU Kids Online, children were asked about their exposure to sexual images online. Although the number of unwanted exposures in that study of 9–16-year-olds compares to the *Journal of Adolescent Health* meta-analysis, the EU study found that on average across European countries, only one in three of those exposed were bothered by this experience. When dividing by age, younger children were more bothered by sexual exposure than teens and those uncomfortable feelings lingered longer (Livingstone et al., 2011). *Why* exactly these children were mostly unbothered is unclear. Perhaps the teens who had more exposure were just used to more sexual content? Maybe as they became more sexually mature, nudity and bodies were normalized? There could also be cultural issues at play with different countries and cultures viewing nudity differently.

This section will cover risks and research, harms and hyperbole. There are real problems with sex on the Internet, but it is not a clear black-and-white issue. Every child is an individual and some have more risk factors than others. Shutting down the Internet and only focusing on the problems does not help our growing and sexually maturing adolescents.

Sexting

Sexting is the sending, receiving, and forwarding of explicit imagery, photos, messages, and others between connected devices. It's a topic that brings up strong feelings with parents and caregivers. There is the social/emotional and youth development side of sexting, and the legal side. This section will discuss both sides and offer some research-driven strategies for parents.

Sexting a topic that frequently comes up in the media, and one that parents are concerned about. Here is a sampling of article titles from 2020 that are representative of much of the media on the topic:

"My teen is sexting!"

—*Family Online Safety Institute*

"The dangers of teen sexting"

—*Pittsburgh Parent*

"Wausau man accused of raping underage relative, sexting"

—*Wausau Daily Herald*

"Snapchat and Teen Vogue Encouraging Teens to Create Child Pornography"

—*National Center on Sexual Exploitation*

Sexting is growing with adolescents. In a national sample from the Cyberbullying Research Center, researchers found an increase of middle and high school students sending and receiving nude photos from a study in 2016. In 2019, approximately 14% of teens

The dangers of teen sexting

March 17, 2020 by Kerri Lutz

By Dr. Gail M. Gross

Recently, I was interviewed by Ashley Johnson at Houston Fox Media concerning the danger of teens using live streaming apps. Since then, I have been thinking about not just the potential dan-

Figure 5.1 Article about the dangers of teen sexting

had sent and 23% had received sexually explicit images (Hinduja, 2020). While this number is not insignificant, it's not the percentage media headlines might have you believe. It is unclear from data if the increase in sexting may be due to reasons such as the increase in mobile phone ownership, not necessarily more teens sexting.

Yes, many teens are sexting, but many are not. Sexting is often looked at as a problem, but what if it's a symptom of something else? Why do young people sext? Table 5.1 summarizes motives why teens sext and what to do about it. According to the Cyberbullying Research Center other reasons teens cite as why they sext include:

- Curiosity
- Boredom
- Pressure/coercion in a relationship
- Hormones and sexual desire
- Experimentation with sexual identity
- Desire to get closer to a partner
- Affirmation and attention
- Accident

(Hinduja, 2020)

Some of these reasons are natural and normal parts of teen development. Others are related to externals like being in a relationship, not turning off a webcam, or peer pressure. If we look at this list through the lens of prevention science we can examine individual, family, and community protective factors to prevent some of the negatives of sexting.

There are some positive consequences of teens sexting. Some researchers and studies suggest that the decline in teen pregnancy rates since the 2000s is a direct result of the Internet (Guldi and Herbst, 2016). A review of qualitative literature in 2017 studied the "small but emerging field of qualitative research" that found for many young people sexting is fun and a part of sexual experimentation for teens who are not ready to engage in physical activity (Anastassiou, 2017). Discussions on sexting are often top-down, with adults imposing their opinions and values on the teens. To a teen who cares about their dating partner, is having fun, and is taking precautions when sexting, this fear may seem overblown and they are less likely to listen to these adults.

Adults need to acknowledge that sexting has some potential positives, not just negatives. They should not frame it in a black-and-white

Table 5.1 Why Do Teens Sext and What to Do About It?

Risk Factor	Suggested Strategy
Curiosity	Curiosity is natural and normal. Direct the teen to evidence-based sexual education.
Boredom	Provide the teen with more opportunities for activities and social interaction such as a team sport, an afterschool program, etc.
Pressure/coercion in a relationship	Teach healthy relationship principles. Also, let teens know that sexting is not as common as they may think.
Hormones and sexual desire	Sexual desire and interest are normal at this age. Direct the teen to evidence-based sexual education.
Experimentation with sexual identity	Experimentation is normal at this age. Encourage, do not shame, the behaviors, and direct them to positive and safe spaces online or in real life.
Desire to get closer to partner	It is normal to want to connect and feel close to a dating partner. However, teaching healthy relationship principles can create some boundaries for these desires.
Affirmation and attention	We all want to be affirmed and get attention. Redirect the sexting to other ways of attention. Evaluate the teen's mental health and your own interactions with them. Are they getting enough attention at home or at school?
Accident	Sometimes photos can be accidentally taken or picked up by a webcam. Make sure that webcams are covered in any teen's laptop.

way, all or nothing, but acknowledge that many teens are sexting and try to guide them. Teens should know both sides.

The other side of sexting involves legal consequences. It's important for educators and parents to share this side, but not in a heavy-handed and fear-based way. Sex educator Shafia Zaloom said, "If you're under eighteen, taking sexually explicit photos of yourself and 'sexting' . . . is considered trafficking in child pornography and is against federal law. Some states have teen sexting laws to deal with this common issue because the consequences for teens who violate federal law can be severe" (Zaloom, 2019). These state laws can vary and the law moves slowly. The consequences can vary depending on what nudes were shared and with how many, the ages of the teens, and more.

"Remember, too, that what is on your device and what you send to others is essentially public," Zaloom continues. "Just because the photos disappear from your phone doesn't mean that someone didn't screenshot and forward or save them" (Zaloom, 2019).

While there are those consequences, parents and educators should be cautious when talking about sexting. A study of sextortion of minors in the *Journal of Adolescent Health* found that fear of the consequences of sexting may make minors feel they are "trapped" after sending an explicit image. This can make them more vulnerable to extortion (Wolak et al., 2018).

Textbox 5.2

Technology plays a key role in sex trafficking, the illegal business of grooming, harboring, acquiring, and transporting people for the purpose of sex. Nonprofit organization Thorn put out a report from studies of survivors of sex trafficking that reported 75% of them were advertised online. More than 150,000 new escort ads are posted online every day ("Child Sex Trafficking Statistics," 2020).

Risk factors for sex trafficking include young people who have been abused, victims of dating violence, and those that don't have social support. Runaway and homeless youth, particularly LGBTQ youth, are at higher risk for becoming victims. Some evidence suggests that LGBTQ youth are more than five times more likely than heterosexuals to be victims of trafficking in part because of isolation, rejection, and being kicked out of the home (U.S. Department of Health and Human Services, 2014).

Some red flags of child sex trafficking victims include:

- Drug addiction
- Uncharacteristic promiscuity beyond age-specific norms
- An older boyfriend or girlfriend
- Attempts to conceal scars or tattoos
- Signs of physical trauma
- Withdrawn behavior, depression, anxiety, or fear
- Unexplained absences from school

- Coached or rehearsed responses to questions
- Change in personal hygiene

Sex trafficking thrives in shame and secrecy. Have open communication about sex and do not shame teens for any mistakes they may make. The best way you can protect your children is to help them feel safe, loved, and supported.

Researchers out of the Cyberbullying Research Center recommend "safe sexting." They write, "Generally speaking, emphasizing avoidance of risky sexual behaviors via abstention has proven ineffectual. . . . It is time to move beyond abstinence-only, fear-based sexting education (or worse yet, no education at all)" (Hinduja, 2020). What does safe sexting look like? This type of education provides knowledge and skills. It's not about encouraging sex but also does not discourage sexual curiosity.

Some of the themes recommended in the Cyberbullying Research Center's December 2019 *Journal of Adolescent Health* article are paraphrased here:

- Trust those to whom you send sexts.
- Do not share sexts you are sent with anyone else.
- Consider sending suggestive pictures instead of nudes.
- Never include your face in a sext and be careful not to send pictures that can identify you through birthmarks, tattoos, or your surroundings in the picture.
- If you are being pressured or threatened to send nude photos, collect digital evidence.
- Delete explicit photos and videos from your device (Hinduja, 2020).

There are legitimate concerns about adolescents sexting. But we as parents, mentors, and educators need to understand the WHYs of teen sexting, and make sure our approach and response is fair, calm, and collaborative.

Pornography

Pornography is a huge part of the Internet. The site Pornhub, the world's most visited pornography website, reported in their 2019

Table 5.2 Risk and Protective Factors for Pornography Consumption

Risk Factors	Protective Factors	Domain
Family conflict, family history of pornography use	Family connectedness	Family
Availability of pornographic materials	Programs that support healthy norms such as internet safety presentations	Community
Experienced child abuse	Positive parenting style	Individual
Peers/friends who engage in pornography	Positive peer role models	Individual
Low caregiver monitoring or frequent coercive discipline	Positive parenting style	Family
Male	Female	Individual
Little or no attachment to school	Positive and close attachments to school	Community

Year in Review that there were over 42 billion visits to the site that year (Wikipedia, 2020; Pornhub, 2019). Also, that year there were a "record amount of video uploads, over 6.83 million new videos were uploaded to Pornhub. To put that in perspective—if you strung all of 2019's new video content together and started watching in 1850, you'd still be watching them today!" (Pornhub, 2019).

For growing and changing adolescents, pornography can become a big part of their lives, and influence their development of their own digital identity. It can also impact the way they view relationships, other genders, and how their bodies are supposed to look.

What are the risk and protective factors of pornography? A systematic review of the literature through 2005 through 2016 by faculty with Brigham Young University (BYU) found several in their research summarized in Table 5.2 (Varner et al., 2017).

In their research they found that boys are more likely to use pornography. Boys, in particular those aged 13–15, should be targeted with sex education (Varner et al., 2017). Sex educator Shafia Zaloom has worked with boys on this topic:

> When I talk to boys about where their ideas about sex and what it should look like come from, it usually comes down to media and their friends' boasts about their own sexual exploits, which are also typically influenced by media, mostly

porn. Pornography sex largely reflects traditional gender norms of dominance and control, of course, so a boy's conversations about sex don't include their partners' experience but focus instead on cultural expectations of sexual conquest and endurance.

(Zaloom, 2019)

Adolescent consumption, particularly by males, leads to increased belief in traditional, and toxic, gender norms. A literature review of pornography from 1995 to 2015 published in the *Journal of Sex Research* found that pornography consumption is associated with adherence to gender-stereotypical beliefs, and a higher likelihood of boys to engage in sexual aggression (Peter and Valkenburg, 2016).

Girls, although they consume less pornography, are also impacted. Qualitative research on anal sex in heterosexual relationships published in 2014 by Marston and Lewis interviewed teens on how they felt during sex. They found two themes: that coercive tactics were normalized and the normalization of pain and discomfort for women. One interviewee commented, "I just wasn't into it. He didn't seem to care. I wasn't getting aroused by it at all . . . it was just painful" (Marston and Lewis, 2014).

These themes tie in with other basic themes of hetero-normative pornography. These include:

- All women want sex from all men.
- Men are the sexual subject and women the sexual object.
- Women want all types of sex acts from men, even if they are aggressive or humiliating.
- If a woman resists sex, she can be persuaded to change her mind.

Parents should keep in mind the gendered effects of pornography. Boys may feel their penis needs to be a certain size and that going longer or harder makes them more of a man. They may feel pressure to brag about their sexual exploits. Girls may feel that their own sexual pleasure and feelings are not as important as the boy's. They may feel they can't say no and pain is just part of sex. For both genders, pornography creates false expectations about sex and how to look and act during sexual activity. It is typically presented through the male gaze and should be thought of as a performance, not reality. But young people, who may not have much information on sex education, may see these performances as reality.

Sex education can help to present a realistic view of sexual activity. This type of education is supported by the American Medical Association, the American Academy of Pediatrics, and many more organizations. Unfortunately, sex education or the type of programming can vary state by state or school district by school district. Planned Parenthood publishes stats on the state of sex education in the US. Currently, twenty-four states and the District of Columbia mandate sex education. This is a decrease from the past (Planned Parenthood, 2020). A study out of the Guttmacher Institute found that the percentage of teens who received formal education has declined since 2006. The type of formal education has changed as well. For example, the number of teen girls who were taught about consent has declined as well as the number of teens receiving information about birth control (Lindberg et al., 2016).

"Porn is pervasive in our culture . . . in fact, porn has become America's default sex education," said Zaloom:

> Many teens aren't getting adequate sex education in school, and their parents aren't talking to them about it either. As a result, they are turning to porn to satisfy their very natural and healthy curiosity, but that's like watching *The Fast and the Furious* to learn how to drive.
>
> (Zaloom, 2019)

Do not wait or hope that your child's school has formal sex education. Even if it does, it may not be sufficient. Parents need to take the lead on discussing sex, and not leave that role up to online porn.

Examining risk and protective factors of pornography, what can parents and educators do? After summarizing the risk and factors, researchers recommended these solutions:

- Targeting males to discuss frequent internet use
- Peer health education
- Involving students in activities to form a connection to the school
- Attending an Internet safety presentation
- Improving family management
- Filtering or blocking software in the community (Varner et al., 2017)

Textbox 5.3

The misogyny in pornography affects queer bodies and reinforces unhealthy relationship structures. Jess Stahle works closely with parents of LGBTQ+ youth and describes what they experience. "With our youth there is a really big drive towards hentai and anime in general, so it's like the fetishization of the queer body is a massive issue."

Hentai is anime and manga pornography and it can appear in games called *eroge*. It is animated or cartoon-like instead of with flesh-and-blood people. Hentai is known to exaggerate parts of the body such as larger breasts and penises and fetishizes bodies and sexual acts. It is extremely popular; in 2017 Pornhub reported the top search term in the US was "hentai."

"A lot of times queer folks in pornography are viewed through this exploitative lens," said Stahle. "One thing that comes up is more like female-presenting men or the person who is sub in porn, the way that is portrayed is really negatively, like their all power is removed, and this is not just in a BDSM environment."

Stahle also sees positives in hentai and pornography, saying, "It's OK to have a critical lens about the problematic gender roles, while still appreciating the artwork as a whole." The growth of online pornography has also created more opportunities for the LGBTQ+ community to make it their own. "So much of the more empowering pornography is coming through LGBTQ plus channels, there's some beautiful artistic porn. . . . It offers a space for people who are in marginalized populations to kind of take control of their own story. Like you can honestly tell a queer creator a lot of the time because it does have a stronger feminist lens and is more supportive of queer bodies" (Rogers-Whitehead, 2020, interview with Jess Stahle).

Jess Stahle encourages discussions of pornography beyond just talking about its existence or harms. She feels that parents should have discussions that not all pornography is created equal. Some directors and actors work to make more realistic and respectful videos. There are issues to consider when consuming porn such as creators that pay fair wages and protect their actors' health.

Some school districts and countries are providing pornography sex education. For example, a porn literacy program in Boston provided a nine-part media literacy curriculum on pornography for adolescents and was pilot-tested with five classrooms. The program "was designed to change beliefs about, for example, performing in pornography being an easy way to become wealthy, or pornography being realistic" (Rothman et al., 2020). It used a nonjudgmental approach to sexual behaviors and interests and was not designed to stop pornography use. They found in the program that the adolescents who participated in the program experienced "changes in knowledge, attitudes, and behavioral intensions related to pornography" and they found that it did not increase any consumption of pornography by the students" (Rothman et al., 2020).

Young people should think critically about what they consume and the effects on others and themselves. Pornography can cause harm, but often those harms are exaggerated. Greater harms can be the shame that young people experience by consuming pornography. Negative outcomes of pornography are related to the individual's identity. A study published in 2017 in the *Journal of Sex Research* found that those who define themselves as religious were more likely to overestimate the harm and shame and experience greater distress related to their porn consumption and were more likely to call themselves "addicts" (Leonhardt et al., 2017). The study supported further results that support the idea that it's not pornography use, but the belief in harms and shame around that use that exacerbates anxiety and depression. If one believes that pornography is inherently bad, they are more likely to experience shame. But if a person can examine pornography through a critical lens and see more nuance, then they are less likely to feel anxious and distressed about their use (Leonhardt et al., 2017).

Teen Mental Health and Technology

Like with sexting, the debate about adolescent mental health and technology use is heated. While there are mixed or nuanced headlines about social media and adolescents, like with sexting, most skew negative. Here is a sampling of headlines from 2020:

"Social Media & Teens: No Simple Answers"
—Dana Foundation

"Social Media Use May Mess With Teen's Sleep"
—Thrive Global

"Social Media Use Linked to Anxiety, Depression Among Teens, New Study Finds"

—*WBUR News*

"How social media is having unintended consequences on teen mental health"

—*Channel 6 News, Richmond*

From our research with Digital Respons-Ability we have found that the majority of teens we work with report that social media makes them feel better about themselves. In 2019 we surveyed over 2,000 students in grades 7–12. Their responses are in Figure 5.2 with the darker color answering the question, "Does social media make you feel better about yourself?" Our findings support what Common Sense Media found in a national 2020 survey of over a thousand 13–17-year-olds in the United States. "Teens are much more likely to say social media has a positive rather than a negative effect on how they feel," the survey

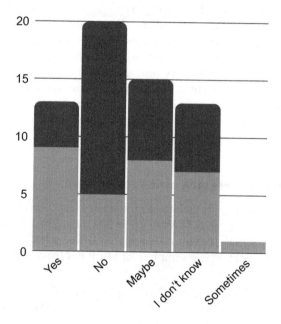

Figure 5.2 Data From Digital Respons-Ability From Teens About How They Feel About Social Media

reported ("Social Media, Social Life Infographic: Common Sense Media," 2020).

This is a different narrative than what we hear when we teach parents. Perhaps it's related to the population; parents who are concerned about their child's technology use are more likely to show up to a class. And perhaps it's the students that are already more depressed who are using social media the most. It could also be the media creating a story around teens and technology. There is mixed research coming from different places.

"It's complicated," said Senior Director of Research from Common Sense Media, Michael Robb:

> There's clearly been an increase in anxiety and depression and other aspects of social and emotional development the last few years. Some people think that it's because of smartphones and the rise of social media. The research shows that excessive use of social media is associated with negative outcomes. But it's not sure what direction that goes.
>
> (Rogers-Whitehead, 2020, interview with Michael Robb)

Robb says one reason the research is unclear is that much of these studies are time use studies. They measure the amount of time a teen is on social media, not necessarily *how* they are using it. This is an issue in screen time research which will be explored more in Chapter 6.

That 2020 Common Sense Media survey asked teens about their own mental health and their social media use. They found that "teens with low social-emotional well-being experience more of the negative effects of social media than kids with high social-emotional well-being" ("Social Media, Social Life Infographic: Common Sense Media," 2020). This may be because teens who feel emotionally low may use social media differently. They may be more passive and lurk rather than comment or post. If they do post, they may post more depressed or sad things that could get negative feedback.

However, it's important to keep in mind that these links and relationships are just one part of what affects a person. Prevention science teaches us there are many risk factors and potentialities for negative feelings and behavior. It's never just one thing that causes the behavior. It's also important not to confuse correlation and causation. Just because there's a link between social media use and behavior does not mean social media caused the behavior.

Robb said, "When they do find the relationships between social media use and negative mental health the relationships they find tend to be quite small. Small enough that you might not think it's worth mentioning. But part of that is our measurement is not particularly good." We need more research in this area. We need more longitudinal studies that go beyond time spent on social media. "You can look at a kid who plays 10 hours a day on video games and he's playing with his friend and he's totally fine socially and emotionally. And you can have another kid who plays 10 hours on the video game and they don't leave the room," said Robb. We need to shift our conversations on kid's technology use how long they are using it, to just *how*. And we need to calm our fears and calm our headlines (Rogers-Whitehead, 2020, interview with Michael Robb).

Social media also has positive effects on mental health. If a parent or caregiver is so concerned about the potential for a small degree of harm that they ban all social media, they can inadvertently end up causing more harm. "As much as there's been a focus on the harmful effects of social media, I think there's been an underappreciation of how important it is for kids to be able to access resources that support themselves online," said Robb (Rogers-Whitehead, 2020, interview with Michael Robb).

Textbox 5.4

Technology impacts genders differently. Social media in particular has been found to affect girls more. A 2018 study in *BMC Public Health* found "stark differences" between teen and tween girls that used social media versus boys. The researchers wrote that "worse well-being was associated with greater social media interaction at age 10" in girls. The earlier girls got into social media, particularly in those tween ages when puberty hits, the worse the girls rated their mental health. The study of girls 10–15 found that "greater interaction on social media at age 10 was associated with worsening socio-emotional difficulties with age among females" (Booker et al., 2018).

Why are girls impacted by social media more? The researchers are not saying that social media causes these impacts, but exacerbates existing conditions and stresses with their developmental stage. They theorize, "It is possible that as adolescent females age there is an increase in upward social comparison leading to decreases in well-being." But it is difficult to say for sure.

Parents should monitor their daughters on social media and have discussions about the messages the media and their friends may send. Girls should know that there are different tools and filters that can create a false idea of beauty or other ideals.

There are some amazing resources for young people online. But there are some pockets and corners of the Internet that parents should watch out for. Remember, it's less important how many hours a teen is online, but what they are doing in those hours.

Echo Chambers Online and Digital Identities

Pornography and sexting are issues with adolescents. But so many educators, watchdogs, and parents focus on the *content* of those issues, not the *context*. Part of the reason that type of media consumption and activity is problematic is that teens don't have a basis in sex education or understand what a healthy relationship looks like. That means the porn they see comes without explanation or context. They don't realize what's real and what's fantastical and what is a harmful message. They are new to relationships and don't have the context for what a healthy relationship looks like. They may assume that sexting or sending nudes is normal. They may think that ALL women should enjoy sex and ALL men should dominate women in sexual acts. They may accept the myth that everyone around them is doing these things, when they're actually not.

Adolescents are figuring out the world and themselves. They are starting more from scratch, with limited experience and life lessons. Their experiences with other people and ideas may be limited to their classmates, soccer team, church group, gamer friends, and other smaller groups. They are lacking context for the world and its ideas.

This lack of context is an issue in certain online forums and pockets. A young person who is building their identity and lacks experience may pick up certain toxic ideas and messages as they build their own identity.

For example, consider the Red Pill movement popular on Reddit, blogs, podcasts, and conventions hosted by 21 Studios. The phrase *red pill* comes from the film *The Matrix* in which Neo, the protagonist, is offered a choice of a red pill, which would reveal to him the truth of the world, or a blue pill, which would return him into happy ignorance. The Red Pill movement, part of the men's rights movement, co-opted that analogy, teaching men that women secretly run the world and society is set up against men.

This can be an appealing idea to teen boys who may feel rejected by girls, berated by teachers or mothers, or just feeling left out. There are statistics that support that life can be hard for men. For example, suicide rates are three to four times higher in the Western world for men than women (Suicide Statistics, 2020). Manufacturing and other male-dominated jobs have declined, while service or other fields like nursing have increased. A teen boy may feel left out or discouraged; those feelings are valid. Unfortunately, those valid feelings can be twisted and co-opted by false and damaging ideas.

The Red Pill movement does not just advocate men's rights, it is a philosophy. This philosophy can be stated thusly: "Life is not fair for men. Women get away with things they shouldn't." The Red Pill philosophy then offers guides and strategies for playing the dating game. They share these strategies to other men so they can cheat at this unfair game that they have to play. If a young teen started viewing these strategies, some may make sense to them. There is advice such as getting healthier and losing weight. But below the surface there is an ideology behind those strategies and pickup-style tips. Women are just seen as trophies or awards, not people. They are what you get for winning the game, not someone to respect or care about. A quick glance below the surface of Red Pill ideology reveals deep misogyny. A Red Pill post on Reddit was titled: "Don't feel guilty about manipulating women: they do it to you already."

This community on Reddit is quarantined for a reason, with a warning label. But anyone can click through that label to access reams of theory, strategy, and misogyny. Red Pill is just one part of the "manosphere" and other misogynist echo chambers online. There are other toxic corners where a vulnerable adolescent, figuring out their way in the world, can be influenced. For example, boards on 4chan, the anonymous messaging board site, contain deep misogyny, porn, and the alt-right movement thru boards like / pol (politically incorrect).

Other places where these types of hate and echo chambers live are certain private servers on Discord. Discord is a platform that was originally designed for video gaming communities that runs on different channels with text, images, and video. Users can create password-protected or moderated servers that only certain people can have access to. Since its release in 2015, Discord has gained over 250 million unique users and there are chats on topics far beyond video gaming (Rogers-Whitehead, 2018). In 2020, due to a large part because of the COVID-19 pandemic, Discord has grown even more. Another growth on Discord in 2020 has been reports of harassment. Between January and June 2020 Discord received 235,000 reports compared to 128,000 between June and December 2019 (Whittaker, 2020).

While most channels on Discord are related to gaming or pop culture and can be entertaining and supportive, there are some that are toxic. For example, the Charlottesville alt-right rally in 2017 was planned on Discord. While this group and other alt-right communities were banned on Discord, many remain (Roose, 2017).

Teens can create positive and proactive digital identities, or unhappy and toxic ones. Part of that depends on their own internal states and how they consume media. Let's say a teenage boy's girlfriend broke up with him. He feels lonely, sad, and angry at her for rejecting him. He's browsing online and starts hearing messages that make him feel better. He's hearing that the world is against him, it's not *his* fault she broke up with him, women are just that way. He starts reading more, then posting, then taking those ideas into real life. Girls are vulnerable to silos as well. Picture a teen girl who has developed quickly and feels awkward in her growing body. She may get comments from her peers about her appearance. She starts to look on Instagram so she knows what she should be wearing and how she should be looking. She feels insecure and wants help. She, like the boy, gets messages on how she should look. Endless scrolling internalizes those messages, and she starts adjusting her makeup and clothes to fit what she thinks she should look like.

The solution to these toxic echo chambers that can attract and influence teens isn't to ban all technology. It's to educate and offer alternative ideas and norms. It's to show the girl that there are many ways to look and dress. It's teaching the boy to redirect his anger into something positive like a sport or being with his real-life friends. Even adults who spend too much time in one place with everyone saying the same thing will be influenced. This is even more true for teens who don't have the same knowledge and context as adults.

Red Flag Behaviors

It is difficult to know what adolescents are doing behind a screen. Platforms are closed off, password protected, moderated; messages disappear; and there are new and changing apps adults typically are not familiar with. This can cause anxiety in adults, not knowing exactly what's going on. With regular communication and trust, that anxiety can lessen. However, adolescents with higher risk factors or a history of issues online should be monitored more closely. While parents may not know everything behind a screen, they can get a sense of what's going on through red flag behaviors. These are behaviors that should send a signal to parents and caregivers that something is up. That something may not be a tech issue, it can be something else, but they should be an early warning system.

Michael Robb tells parents to look for these behaviors or "clues." He describes some of these clues as "homework is slipping and they aren't doing the other things you know are important for kids like sleeping well, getting good nutrition, or if they are getting physical conditions like stomachaches" (Rogers-Whitehead, 2020, interview with Michael Robb).

Other red flag behaviors include:

- Increased media consumption that goes along with less time on hobbies and activities they used to enjoy
- Repeatedly refusing to join the family at designated family times
- Anger and/or tantrums when devices are taken away
- Silence about online use
- Wanting to access credit cards or money regularly for online activities
- Tiredness and moodiness

Mental health is an issue with adolescents. Their bodies and sleep cycles are changing. They are beginning to date and developing identity. They have pressures and influences from peers, media, school, and more. Technology can be a tool that helps or hinders in these years. But it's important to keep in mind that tech use is just one part of the equation; a symptom, not necessarily a problem. Parents should monitor and mentor, not ban and berate. Your teen needs you.

Digital Branding

When adults talk to young people about technology, it's often through a negative lens.

"You're on your phone too much, what are you doing?"
"Don't go on that website!"

"Why are you wasting your time online?"
"When will you stop gaming?"
"You like those videos?"

Young people get these messages from their parents, teachers, the media, and more. They may get the misconception that the Internet is a waste of time, a place for goofing off, porn is around every corner, and games are for lazy people. There are legitimate concerns for youth online; this book has described many of them. However, if we only frame our discussions and conversations in a negative lens, then that truly does not prepare our children for the future.

As children age into teens, the conversations we have with them need to shift. There are legitimate reasons to filter and be more restrictive for young children, but those reasons fade away as they enter high school. Teens need to know how to use the Internet and technology to navigate information, to communicate well, and more. If they are banned or restricted from devices and the Internet, they do not get an opportunity to develop these skills. They need to develop their digital identities and their digital brand. Employers and college admissions counselors will be seeking them out: what will they find?

College and Career Readiness

What are employers looking for? LinkedIn reported on the most important skills needed in 2020 based on data from their network of 660 million users and 20-plus million job postings. They divided these skills into hard skills and soft skills (Pate, 2020). Soft skills are interpersonal skills while hard skills are teachable skills that are easier to quantify. Both hard skills and soft skills can be learned and nurtured online, although in different ways.

The soft skills LinkedIn listed for 2020 are, in order:

1. Creativity
2. Persuasion
3. Collaboration
4. Adaptability
5. Emotional intelligence

(Pate, 2020)

Four out of five of these skills were the same as 2019. The only difference is "time management," which was the number-five skill in

2019 (Petrone, 2019). The top ten hard skills listed in their 2020 recommendations is full of tech-related topics: blockchain, cloud computing, artificial intelligence, UX Design, affiliate marketing, video production, and more. Their report states, "Many of these skills will continue to evolve rapidly"; however, soft skills are more stable year to year (Pate, 2020).

How exactly can technology encourage those soft skills needed for students to succeed at work?

- *Creativity.* The Internet offers a wealth of free software and apps to create. It has platforms to showcase writing, art, videos, photography, cooking, making, and more. Unlike previous generations, young people now have a surplus of ideas, templates, patterns, recipes, instructional videos, and more to showcase their creativity.
- *Persuasion.* Any time you post or share something on social media, you are persuading your followers to like, follow, share, or comment on it. Being able to persuade through text, videos, photos, and reasoning is important for any career.
- *Collaboration.* There are many opportunities and tools for collaboration online. For example, Citizen Science is the US government's way to enable public participation in science issues (CitizenScience.gov, 2020). You can search for projects near your home, measure water levels, track heat levels, observe biodiversity, and much more. Young people can collaborate and communicate with people across the world in easier ways than ever before.
- *Adaptability.* The fast pace of technology means that students and future workers will need to be flexible and adapt quickly. Being able to navigate different platforms, online tools, and more helps you pivot and change in your working career.
- *Emotional intelligence.* Emotional intelligence is the ability to identify and then manage one's own emotions, and others'. It's a crucial, and hard to measure, skill that is needed to work in and across teams with colleagues and classmates. The Internet can expose young people to different values, beliefs, communication styles, cultures, and more. This exposure can help them become more empathetic, reevaluate their own feelings, and more.

Sometimes adults don't see the skill-building inherent in typical Internet use. An adult who just sees their teen talking to friends all the time may not see persuasion in their communication, or creativity through making or sharing memes or Snaps. There is learning going on through this tech use. Skills built through gaming will be described in a later chapter.

Textbox 5.5

For two years when teaching digital citizenship classes to K-12 students, Digital Respons-Ability measured STEM interest. We found a link between digital citizenship education and interest in STEM. After learning more digital citizenship principles such as online privacy, communication, digital commerce, digital law, online safety, and more, young people expressed more interested in getting into a STEM-related career.

Figure 5.3 is a chart from a group of high school students at a detention facility in 2018. Digital Respons-Ability has worked closely with youth in custody since 2017. After taking a series of digital citizenship classes, their interest in STEM and tech-related careers increased.

The conversations parents have around these topics can not only keep their children safer and more responsible, they can encourage them to seek out those types of careers.

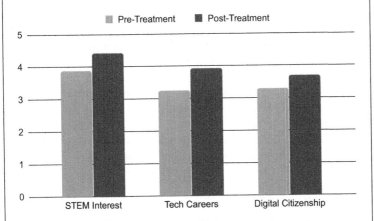

Figure 5.3 Pre and Post Results From Digital Respons-Ability About the Effects of Digital Citizenship Education With Youth in Custody

Creation Versus Consumption

Social media use and screen time are often viewed as one mono-lithic time use. This skews what's actually happening. It's the *hows* of screen and tech use we should be concerned about. If we worry too much about usage in general, we can inadvertently end up hurt-ing ourselves. A 2018 Career Builder survey found that "47% of employers said they wouldn't call a person for an interview if they can't find them online." When the employers were asked further, "20% say it's because they expect candidates to have an online presence" (Driver, 2018). Are we so worried about safety and screen time that we hobble our kids from creating a digital brand?

The summer of 2018 I taught a business class to female inmates at Utah State Prison. My students were very intelligent and eager to learn. However, many expressed frustration and sadness about when they would get out of prison, and what their employers would find online. These students had felonies, and there were media reports, postings on social media, and more on their crimes. Some of their mugshots were what you would find when looking up their names. How can they change such a negative digital brand?

When we talked about technology in terms of business we dis-cussed this issue in depth. I empathized with them; it isn't fair, but it's the world we live in. Our mistakes can follow us online. But we can push back. By creating our own content, our own identities, we can counter the narrative that algorithms create for us. I told the class that if they can push some of that negative press or details back even just to the second page of Google, people may never find it. So what are ways you can create that content?

- *LinkedIn.* Most recruiters and employers check LinkedIn. This digital resume and portfolio will often pop to the top of an algorithm.
- *ePortfolios.* Create a space to showcase your work. Perhaps you love photography. Create an online gallery attached to your gallery. Compile your poetry in a blog. Take your hobby and share it.
- *Write.* Write an op-ed or compose a letter to the editor. Com-ment on media with your name. An intelligent and well-thought-out argument attached to your name can showcase that persuasion skill.

Table 5.3 Consumption Versus Creation

Consumption	Creation
Scrolling through Instagram	Posting a picture on Instagram that means something to you
Anonymously posting on a message board	Responding with your name and identity to a blog or online article
Watching videos on YouTube	Creating your own video
Reading articles about the environment	Being a #citizenscientist and sharing what is happening in your community
Watching anime	Drawing a picture of your favorite character or creating a story about them
Playing a mobile game by yourself	Playing an online game with your friends

Unfortunately, as with the inmates, teens' mistakes may follow them online. I've also taught juveniles in detention and even though they are minors, there are postings about them online with their crimes. Even teens without a criminal history may find their mistakes and goof-ups online for everyone to see. Teens do not have a safe space to make mistakes as their parents did when they were that age. This is why digital citizenship education is so vital, as is a discussion of digital branding.

If you shift your Internet use from consumption to creation, you make that positive digital footprint that can follow you and help others find you. Here are some differences in Table 5.3 between simply consuming content online and creating it. These creations also develop soft skills.

Instead of chiding a child, "You're on YouTube too much," a parent can say, "How about you make a video to post on YouTube?" Or say, "Why don't you stream some of your games?" instead of, "You play too many online games." During the teen years parents need to restrict less and encourage more. These teens are already applying for jobs and colleges. They will be out of the house soon. Are they digitally ready?

Strategies for Communicating With Your Teen

Annabel Sheinberg is the VP of Learning and Partnerships with Planned Parenthood of Utah. She has experience talking to parents and teens on sensitive topics. Sheinberg suggests when talking to teens to be vulnerable and open. Treat them respectfully and "try to be collaborative and empathetic in your approach." She goes onto recommend parents "engage in mutual problem solving when possible rather than using the 'parent voice.' This will deepen your relationship and connection so that future conversations happen" (Rogers-Whitehead, 2020, interview with Annabel Sheinberg).

Here are some conversation starters for talking to teens about technology:

- What do you think that (show/movie/meme etc.) is trying to say? Why do you think it's saying that?
- What would you tell a friend who shared something online that probably should have been kept private?
- If a friend told you that you shared something that should have been private, or made them feel uncomfortable, how would you feel?
- How does technology affect dating relationships? What do you see?
- What's something positive you can do online today?
- Who do you want to be online?

Who am I? Who do I want to be online? These are questions adolescents are asking themselves as they do necessary work of developing their real-life and digital identities. Parents can be a vital source of strength, comfort, and advice as they work through texts and temptations that will test and challenge them.

Summary Points: Digital Identities

- Puberty completes during the late teen years. Teens become sexually and physically mature.
- Teens are forming their identities, both in real life and digitally. Peers, media, and spaces online can influence that identity-forming.
- Sexting is the sending, receiving, and forwarding of explicit imagery, photos, messages, and others between connected devices. Sexting is growing with teens. Sexting has both pros and cons.

- Male adolescents are more likely to consume pornography. Pornography reflects and promotes traditional and toxic gender norms.
- Twenty percent of adolescents will have unwanted sexual exposure online. Sex and Internet safety education and regular communication can help prevent unhealthy pornography use, sexting, and other unhealthy sexual behaviors online.
- Social media does not cause depression and anxiety. However, teens who are already depressed and anxious may have their moods affected negatively by social media.
- Lack of context and life experiences are risk factors for teenagers. This means they may be highly influenced by toxic and false echo chambers online.
- Parents should monitor teens' behaviors and moods and encourage good physical habits like regular sleep.
- As teens approach adulthood, parents should shift conversations on technology to how it can be used to create content, showcase a positive digital identity, apply for jobs, and find colleges.

References

Anastassiou, Andrea. "Sexting and Young People: A Review of the Qualitative Literature." *Qualitative Report* 22 (2017): 8–16.

Booker, C.L., Y.J. Kelly, and A. Sacker. "Gender Differences in the Associations between Age Trends of Social Media Interaction and Well-Being among 10–15 Year Olds in the UK." *BMC Public Health* 18, no. 321 (2018). https://doi.org/10.1186/s12889-018-5220-4.

"Child Sex Trafficking Statistics." *Thorn*, January 17, 2020. www.thorn.org/child-trafficking-statistics/.

CitizenScience.gov. www.citizenscience.gov/ (Accessed April 13, 2020).

Driver, Saige. "Social Media Screenings Gain in Popularity." *Business News Daily*, October 7, 2018. www.businessnewsdaily.com/2377-social-media-hiring.html.

Ferguson, Christopher. Conversation with the author March 2020.

Guldi, Melanie, and Chris M. Herbst. "Offline Effects of Online Connecting: The Impact of Broadband Diffusion on Teen Fertility Decisions." *Journal of Population Economics* 30 no. 1 (2016): 69–91. https://doi.org/10.1007/s00148-016-0605-0.

Hinduja, Sameer. "It Is Time to Teach Safe Sexting." *Cyberbullying Research Center*, January 16, 2020. https://cyberbullying.org/it-is-time-to-teach-safe-sexting.

Leonhardt, Nathan D., Brian J. Willoughby, and Bonnie Young-Petersen. "Damaged Goods: Perception of Pornography Addiction as a Mediator between Religiosity and Relationship Anxiety Surrounding Pornography Use." *The Journal of Sex Research* 55, no. 3 (2017): 357–368. https://doi.org/10.1080/00224499.2017.1295013.

Lindberg, Laura Duberstein, Isaac Maddow-Zimet, and Heather Boonstra. "Changes in Adolescents' Receipt of Sex Education, 2006–2013." *Journal of Adolescent Health* 58, no. 6 (2016): 621–627. https://doi.org/10.1016/j.jadohealth.2016.02.004.

Livingstone, Sonia, Leslie Haddon, Anke Görzig, and Kjartan Ólafsson. "Risks and Safety on the Internet: The Perspective of European Children: Full Findings and Policy Implications from the EU Kids Online Survey of 9–16 Year Olds and Their Parents in 25 Countries." *EU Kids Online*, Deliverable D4, EU Kids Online Network, London, UK, 2011.

Madigan, Sheri, and Gina Dimitropoulos. "One in Five Youth See Unwanted Sexual Content Online, Says New Research." *The Conversation*, March 26, 2020. https://theconversation.com/one-in-five-youth-see-unwanted-sexual-content-online-says-new-research-96097.

Madigan, Sheri, Vanessa Villani, Corry Azzopardi, Danae Laut, Tanya Smith, Jeff R. Temple, Dillon Browne, and Gina Dimitropoulos. "The Prevalence of Unwanted Online Sexual Exposure and Solicitation Among Youth: A Meta-Analysis." *Journal of Adolescent Health* 63, no. 2 (2018): 133–141. https://doi.org/10.1016/j.jadohealth.2018.03.012.

Marston, Cicely and Lewis, Ruth. "Anal Heterosex among Young People and Implications for Health Promotion: A Qualitative Study from the UK. *BMJ Open* 4 (2014): 1–7. doi:10.1136/bmjopen-2014-004996.

Morin, Amy. "The Developmental Milestones 18-Year-Olds Reach." *Verywell Family*, July 15, 2019. www.verywellfamily.com/18-year-old-developmental-milestones-2609030.

National Research Council (US) and Institute of Medicine (US) Forum on Adolescence, and Kipke, MD, editor. *Adolescent Development and the Biology of Puberty: Summary of a Workshop on New Research*. Washington, DC: National Academies Press (US), 1999. Adolescent Development and the Biology of Puberty. www.ncbi.nlm.nih.gov/books/NBK224692/.

Pate, Deanna. "The Skills Companies Need Most in 2020 and How to Learn Them." *LinkedIn Learning*. https://learning.linkedin.com/blog/top-skills/the-skills-companies-need-most-in-2020-and-how-to-learn-them (Accessed April 13, 2020).

Peter, J., and P.M. Valkenburg. "Adolescents and Pornography: A Review of 20 Years of Research." *The Journal of Sex Research* 53, no. 4–5 (2016): 209–531.

Petrone, Paul. "The Skills Companies Need Most in 2019: And How to Learn Them." *LinkedIn Learning*. https://learning.linkedin.com/blog/top-skills/the-skills-companies-need-most-in-2019-and-how-to-learn-them (Accessed April 13, 2020).

Planned Parenthood. "State of Sex Education in USA: Health Education in Schools." *Planned Parenthood*. www.plannedparenthood.org/learn/for-educators/whats-state-sex-education-us (Accessed April 5, 2020).

Pornhub. "The 2019 Year in Review." December 11, 2019. www.pornhub.com/insights/2019-year-in-review.

"Pornhub." *Wikipedia*. Wikimedia Foundation, May 28, 2020. https://en.wikipedia.org/wiki/Pornhub.

Robb, Michael. Conversation with the author March 2020.

Rogers-Whitehead, Carrie. "The Discord with Discord: What Parents Need to Know about the Popular Gamer Chat." *KSL.com*, December 5, 2018. www.ksl.com/article/46441334/the-discord-with-discord-what-parents-need-to-know-about-the-popular-gamer-chat.

Roose, Kevin. "This Was the Alt-Right's Favorite Chat App. Then Came Charlottesville." *The New York Times*, August 15, 2017. www.nytimes.com/2017/08/15/technology/discord-chat-app-alt-right.html.

Rothman, Emily F., Nicole Daley, and Jess Alder. "A Pornography Literacy Program for Adolescents." *American Journal of Public Health* 110, no. 2 (February 1, 2020): 154–156. https://doi.org/10.2105/AJPH.2019.305468.

Sheinberg, Annabel. Conversation with the author December 2019.

Shroff, Amita. "Puberty and Girls: What to Expect When Girls Hit Puberty." *WebMD*, April 23, 2018. https://teens.webmd.com/girls/facts-about-puberty-girls.

"Social Media, Social Life Infographic: Common Sense Media." Common Sense Media: Ratings, Reviews, and Advice. www.commonsensemedia.org/social-media-social-life-infographic (Accessed April 8, 2020).

Stahle, Jess. Conversation with the author April 2020.

"Suicide Statistics." *American Foundation for Suicide Prevention*, May 14, 2020. https://afsp.org/about-suicide/suicide-statistics/.

U.S. Department of Health and Human Services, Administration for Children, Youth and Families. *Guidance to States and Services on Addressing Human Trafficking of Children and Youth in the United States*. Washington, DC: Author, 2014. www.acf.hhs.gov/sites/default/files/cb/acyf_human_trafficking_guidance.pdf.

Varner, J., K. Hoch, M.C. Goates, and C. Hanson. "Proactive Protection for Adolescents, the Innocent Victim: Risk and Protective Factors for Pornography." Presentation at the *Utah Society of Public Health Educators Annual Conference*, Ogden, UT, September, 2017.

Whittaker, Zack. "Discord says user abuse reports have doubled since last year." *TechCrunch*, August 27, 2020. https://techcrunch.com/2020/08/27/discord-transparency-doubled/

Wolak, Janis, David Finkelhor, Wendy Walsh, and Leah Treitman. "Sextortion of Minors: Characteristics and Dynamics." *Journal of Adolescent Health* 62, no. 1 (2018): 72–79. https://doi.org/10.1016/j.jadohealth.2017.08.014.

Zaloom, Shafia. *Sex, Teens, and Everything in between: The New and Necessary Conversations Today's Teenagers Need to Have about Consent, Sexual Harassment, Healthy Relationships, Love and More.* Naperville, IL: Sourcebooks, 2019.

Chapter 6

Screen Time
The Real Facts and Research

In 2019 my team and I at Digital Respons-Ability taught hundreds of parents in small group digital parenting classes. At the end of the class we had a survey we requested them to fill out with their feedback and their concerns around technology. The three top concerns with their kids all revolved around screen time:

- Spending too much time on screens
- Interacting only with their phone
- Using phone to avoid people

Screen time is the new bogeyman for parents; some may call it a moral panic. I don't use the term "moral panic" to dismiss the concerns of parents I teach. As a parent myself it's something I think about a lot and regulate at home. We *should* be talking about screen time, but we *shouldn't* be obsessing over it. But I do feel that the worries are overblown and both the media and misinformation have fanned the fears of parents. This is understandable because how we measure, evaluate, and look at screen time can vary in research practices and in our perspectives. This chapter seeks to examine the research and the flaws in that research, and look at screen time from a prevention science lens.

Research on Screen Time

Douglas Adams, author of the comedy science fiction series *The Hitchhiker's Guide to the Galaxy*, shares his thoughts on new technology:

> I've come up with a set of rules that describe our reactions to technologies:
>
> 1. Anything that is in the world when you're born is normal and ordinary and is just a natural part of the way the world works.

2. Anything that's invented between when you're fifteen and thirty-five is new and exciting and revolutionary and you can probably get a career in it.

3. Anything invented after you're thirty-five is against the natural order of things.

(Adams, 2002)

The idea of screen time is pretty new. Yes, there were screens before, but there was typically just one or two in the house and you only used one screen at a time. This new concept and technologies may seem, as in Adams's quote, "against the natural order of things." Thus, when the American Academy of Pediatrics (AAP) released the journal article "The Impact of Social Media on Children, Adolescents, and Families" in 2011, people were primed and ready to react (O'Keeffe and Clarke-Pearson, 2011). The article was highly cited and helped release a slew of articles, bloggers, groups, and others stoking fears about screen time.

However, newer research pushes back against the narrative of screen time and social media causing mental health issues. The 2011 article cautions about "Facebook depression" and in 2016 the AAP revised its statement and took out that mention (O'Keeffe and Clarke-Pearson, 2011). A lead author, Megan Moreno, told the *New York Times* that the phrase was problematic "because it created panic without a strong basis of evidence" (Popper, 2020).

Another article that went viral and stirred more panic was Jean Twenge's piece in *The Atlantic* in 2017, "Have Smartphones Ruined a Generation?" (Twenge, 2017). She writes in the article, "The twin rise of the smartphone and social media has caused an earthquake of a magnitude we've not seen in a very long time, if ever. There is compelling evidence that the devices we've placed in young people's hands are having profound effects on their lives—and making them seriously unhappy." In the article Twenge discusses the rise in mental health issues and youth suicides happening at the same time as widescale smartphone adoption. To Twenge, the smartphones cause the problems. But critics note that while there is correlation, there is no evidence of causation. Prevention science teaches us that there are multiple risk factors that affect behavior, not just one. During the time that smartphones became more popular, the economy had a Great Recession, global warming was occurring, prices of college and housing had increased, and there was greater income inequality. There are many reasons young people may be more anxious. Twenge stands by her research even through criticisms, and there is research that can back up that stance. But when you examine the research as a whole, and the research methods, a more complicated picture occurs.

A meta-analysis of about forty surveys published between 2014 and 2019 published in 2020 in the *Journal of Child Psychology and Psychiatry* found "most research to date has been correlational, focused on adults versus adolescents, and has generated a mix of often conflicting small positive, negative and null associations" (Odgers, 2020). Another meta-analysis out of the *Journal of Affective Disorders* in 2019 examined the concept of "Facebook depression" mentioned in the AAP statement. Analysts found that it wasn't necessarily the screen time but "social comparisons" that were more related to depression (Yoon et al., 2019).

What are the issues with research regarding screen time? I saw problems first-hand with some of my research with Digital Respons-Ability. When we first started teaching student classes on digital citizenship, we would survey the students about their screen time usage. In the initial surveys, there was a blank space where students could fill in their answer in hours. We found out quickly that relying on student self-reporting was problematic. We had many sarcastic middle schoolers that would simply write in "24 hours." When trying to get an average amount of screen time it's difficult to calculate with these outliers. Even one answer of "24 hours" is going to skew any data collected.

Then there are also issues of accurate self-reporting. While the vast majority of our students would not write a snarky "24 hour" response to the question, they had difficulty estimating their screen time use. *"Does it count double when you use two screens? What did I do yesterday? If I use a lot of screens on the weekend should I average that in my response?"* We later changed the question and included a definition of screen time and a range of response for them to pick from. Even then, one cannot have perfect accuracy with self-reporting.

There are apps and devices that can record and track screen time. They will be more accurate in self-reporting, but then there are concerns about online privacy, installing apps, and tracking minors. In addition, a screen time app on the phone will just track phone usage; it doesn't count in that TV watched, the time on you're a friend's phone, the time on a game, etc. Much of the research on screen time has relied on flawed and inaccurate pieces of data from trackers or self-reporting. That makes any correlations suspect since it's hard to get a realistic picture of exactly how many hours young people are on screens.

Another issue with research is the nature of self-reporting. Someone may report a positive or negative feeling based on something completely different. They may confuse their feelings of discomfort from hunger with discomfort from their phone. Lisa Feldman Barrett is a researcher and professor of psychology at Northeastern University and studies the science of emotion. She writes in her book *How Emotions are Made: The Secret Life of the Brain* about how the brain constantly makes predictions based on outside stimuli, which turn into feelings:

> Familiar sensations like your heart beating in your chest, your lungs filling with air, and, most of all, the general pleasant, unpleasant, aroused and quiescent sensations of affect are not really coming from inside your body . . . in short, you feel what your brain believes. Affect primarily comes from prediction.
> (Barrett, 2018)

Our feelings are driven by our perceptions of what is around them. Our black box of a brain which cannot "see" outside our body creates predictions based on past experience. Thus, we may misinterpret our feelings and responses to technology because of a cyberbullying incident a few years ago, not getting enough sleep the night before, losing at a video game, feeling sick, or more. While self-reporting is important and a tool in the toolbox of research, we have to take many of these screen time self-reporting studies with a grain of salt. There are many reasons why someone may feel a certain way.

This relates to another issue with research about screen time: the perception that screen time is inherently bad. If you are surveyed on your screen time use, and you have read many reports and media about how it's not good, that will affect your response. If a researcher read the AAP statement and has issues with their own screen time use, they may conduct their research in a biased way. No research is perfect but analyzing existing research around screen time finds little evidence and flawed methodology. We need better research on this topic, and also need the media to better report on less headline-grabbing topics. Instead of *Social media can cause teen suicide,* we need more headlines like *Teen suicide is a complicated, multi-faceted issue that needs more research.*

Prevention Science and Screen Time

Prevention science, as covered in Chapter 2, teaches us that behavior is guided by a variety of different individual, family, and community factors. The media and other hyperbolic studies and reports treat screen time as *the* reason behavior changes. It's more accurate to view screen time as a symptom of another underlying cause. In addition, parents should view screen time as a factor that can potentially create more adverse outcomes to existing conditions. For example, if a child is obese, screen time can potentially make their health worse by encouraging sedentary behaviors. Or if a teen is depressed, screen time can deepen those negative feelings by isolating the teen from hobbies or friends.

An eight-year longitudinal study published in 2020 in *Computers in Human Behavior* examined the screen time on social media and adolescent mental health. The researchers discuss some of the issues with screen time research: "Many studies have found a link between time spent using social media and mental health issues, such as depression and anxiety. However, the existing research is plagued by cross-sectional research and lacks analytic techniques examining individual change over time" (Coyne, 2020). Most screen time research takes a snapshot of behavior. And someone who is hungry, or failed a test, or got a bad night's sleep might report negative behavior based on something entirely different than screen time.

This study of over 500 adolescents tracked them yearly from age 13 and 20 and "results revealed that increased time spent on social media was not associated with increased mental health issues" (Coyne, 2020). Thus, mental health issues are not caused by screen time with social media, they're preexisting.

Another misassumption that's made about screen time is that if children are not behind screens they will automatically be doing some kind of positive, healthy activity. Turning off screens does not necessarily make young children go outside and engage in imaginative play or make an overweight child go running. Screens are one of many sedentary choices that children have. Without a screen a child might decide to draw or play with LEGOs inside. Parents make a false dichotomy between screen time and other activities.

"If he wouldn't play games so much he would go outside more."
"I wish she would get off her phone so she would go back to playing piano."
"The phone is taking her away from her friends."

These statements may be true, but there's no way of knowing. But parents and caregivers treat it as an if/then statement rather than one of many potential possibilities. And why would a child decide to get off games when they don't have an outdoor toy to play with? Maybe the hypothetical girl stopped playing the piano because she didn't enjoy it, not because of the phone. And who's to say that a phone is taking a teen away from their friends? It may be a way to connect with those friends.

It's a reasonable request to limit screens. Screens *can* take children away from other positive activities and are mostly sedentary. But parents need to help make that happen. Simply taking away a screen will not suddenly change the behavior. Provide options and help. Offer a ride to activities. Provide non-screen toys and a safe and fun place to play outside. Set up playdates and drive them to their friend's house. Screen time is an opportunity cost. The more time spent behind screens, the less time for other activities. However, it's not a one-to-one cost with a direct connection, just as it's not a direct connection to depression, anxiety, or other mental health issues. Screens are just one factor, one activity, among many things that children can participate in.

Homework and Screen Time

Online learning is a type of screen time that shouldn't necessarily be included when calculating the number of hours a child is behind a screen. This type of screen time holds many benefits such as personalized learning, which allows educators to better track a student's progress, teaching visually and in different ways, and providing more opportunities for home and non-traditional learning. In addition, homework online is often a necessity for students. Despite its benefits, there are controversies with online learning.

Screen time battles are not just at home but also involve schools. These skirmishes have played out in school districts around the world. In early 2020, parents at Normal Public Schools in Oklahoma came to a school board meeting to voice their complaints. As reported in the Normal Transcript, "Parents presented a wide spectrum of concerns about their children's technology use that spanned from students' increased screen time to in-school pornography exposure" (Keith, 2020). One parent from a school district in Austin, Texas, described to the *Washington Post* her observation of her son's third-grade class: "They were zoned out like little zombies" (Truong, 2020). The *Post* article later states of these parents, "They say that schools are usurping the authority of parents who may limit screen time at home or monitor their children's Internet activity on personal devices" (Truong, 2020).

The debate continues, although it may be different after vast, large-scale online learning due to the COVID-19 quarantine that forced schools to close in 2020. Regardless, there are strong feelings about screen time not just at home, but also in schools.

Part of this debate is due to the quality of online learning, which can vary widely depending on the platform, teacher, student's capabilities, and manner of the technology's use. Merve Lapus, the VP of Outreach and National Partnership with Common Sense Media, describes what he's seeing with online homework during the COVID-19 school closures: "I've heard of many schools who are saying 9–3, 'OK login.' That is an expectation that I personally and professional don't feel is beneficial. There are so many other compounds that you have to think about that are happening there" (Rogers-Whitehead, 2020, interview with Merve Lapus). Online homework, just like educational apps, can be interactive, or simply clicking through or passively watching. Educators may not have extensive training on how to teach online. Instructional design is a different field than teaching and uses different skillsets.

The lack of quality in some online learning may cause additional stress at home. Lapus goes onto say:

> I'm hearing a lot of this from educators. In one week, you expect to reach x amount of lessons to get y amount of outcomes—but you need to cut those expectations in half. . . . You need to simplify, how do you design backwards? What do you want? How can you measure that? Can this digital tool get me there? It's not about replacing the educator it's about understanding how a tool is being used.
> (Rogers-Whitehead, 2020, interview with Merve Lapus)

How can parents decrease stress about homework behind screens? For more tips on homework see Chapter 8.

- *Give breaks.* Both you and your child need a break from home-work. Set a timer for 15–30 minutes or more and have a quick snack break or stretch between assignments.
- *What is optional?* Not all online learning is required in school, some is supplemental. If a supplemental or optional assignment is causing stress or taking up too much time, drop it.
- *Pick the best time.* If it's late and your child needs to get to bed, don't insist on finishing up the online homework. It will just make them more tired the next day and they will not be work-ing at their best. Find the best times during the day and week for homework when kids are rested and not distracted by other activities.

Merve Lapus is also a father of two and has dealt with the pressure of online learning at home:

> You don't want to fill your kids up with 400 different educational resources. Really understand what tools seem to work and how do you leverage that tool for all it could provide. . . . As parents are trying to understand how these tools are working, it can cause more confusion and stress. If your kid is stressed out because they don't understand the content and the tool, now you have a par-ent's stress also not understanding the content and the tool. That leads to more compounding issues that leads to more stress that leads to a degradation of learning. Being cognizant of that and how you're feeling and what your capacity is, means you can nar-row things down to work as a parent and an educator.
>   (Rogers-Whitehead, 2020, interview with Merve Lapus)

Sleep and Screens

The battle for bedtime has been exacerbated by technology. Before, parents may have had to deal with numerous requests for stories and water. Now they deal with numerous requests for a smart-phone. While the research is flawed between screen time and mental health concerns, there is a clearer and more direct link between our screens and sleep.

The US National Institutes of Health are conducting a landmark long-term study on adolescent brain cognitive development, otherwise known as the ABCD study. They have released a large dataset from over 7,500 youth and families which is informing and providing data for researchers around the world. One article that examines that research was published in the *International Journal of Behavioral Nutrition and Physical Activity* in 2019. It focused on how sleep duration could mediate problem behaviors associated with screen time (ST). "The largest effects were observed between sleep duration and all problem behaviors, with greater sleep duration predicting an 8.8–16.6% decrease in problem behaviors," the article stated (Guerrero et al., 2019). Simply, the more sleep an adolescent had, the less they exhibited problem behaviors.

The results of the study pushed back on research behind screen time and problem behaviors: "Our findings on ST and anxiety/depression align with other cross-sectional research documenting null effects." They did find that increased watching of television, playing video games, and watching videos reduced sleep (Guerrero et al., 2019). This relates to opportunity cost: there are only so many hours a day and if you increase one activity, you may decrease another. "As children spend significant time in ST behaviors, it replaces time given to other activities, such as sleep. Furthermore, when children spend time on screens (especially at night) they are exposed to the blue light, which has been shown to delay sleep onset and reduce sleep quality" (Guerrero et al., 2019).

What is this blue light to which the journal article refers? Blue light is a specific range of the light spectrum; it's what makes the sky blue. Most screens emit blue light and when bodies are exposed to blue light at times of the day they should be sleeping, it sends a signal to the brain that it's still daytime. Blue light suppresses melatonin, the chemical that helps the body get ready for sleep (Rogers-Whitehead, 2018). Screens do not just take away our hours, they can also take away the chemicals we need to sleep.

Sleep is a risk factor for many behaviors. You can make a strong argument that if you wanted to stop cyberbullying, the best thing you can do is to make sure adolescents get enough sleep. Lack of sleep deeply affects the brain. Some effects of lack of sleep include:

- Memory loss
- Inability to focus
- Irritability and increased aggression
- Increased risk-taking
- Lower immune responses
- Weight gain

- Higher risks of diabetes and heart issues
- Feelings of depression and anxiety

Another effect is the lack of self-control and emotional regulation. In the book by sleep researcher Matthew Walker, *Why We Sleep: Unlocking the Power of Sleep and Dreams,* he writes, "The coolheaded ability to regulate our emotions a key to what we call emotional IQ—depends on getting sufficient REM sleep night after night" (Walker, 2018).

Psychology lecturer and researcher Jakke Tamminen writes in an article, "Sleep deprived participants in one study experienced greater stress and anger than rested control participants when asked to complete a simple cognitive test" (Tamminen, 2018). Through brain imaging scientists have found that the amygdala, an area deep in the brain which assists in emotional regulation, is highly reactive when sleep-deprived. In a study reported in *Current Biology* in 2007, researchers found that "activity levels in the amygdala were as much as 60% higher than levels in those who were rested" (Yoo, 2007).

This reactivity can cause people to not think before sharing, commenting, posting, or messaging online. The irritability and anxiety caused by tiredness can also mean incorrect interpretations, misassumptions, and taking things personally online. If a tired teen is scrolling their feed late at night they may overreact to a post, make an unkind comment, and then have to deal with the consequences the next morning.

Adolescents in particular are vulnerable to lack of sleep. The National Sleep Foundation reports that "teens need about 8 to 10 hours of sleep each night to function best. Most teens do not get enough sleep—one study found that only 15% reported sleeping 8 ½ hours on school nights" (Sleep Foundation, 2020). Adolescents also have irregular sleep patterns, sleeping less on school days and in excess on the weekends, which affects their biological clocks.

A 2018 study published in the *International Journal of Public Health* analyzed data from four surveys of adolescents between 2002 and 2014. They found that adolescents that had more than two hours of daily screen time "had 20% higher odds of reporting sleep-onset difficulties. . . . The strength of the association between screen time and sleep-onset difficulties increased over time, which may reflect a change in the type of screen time use (e.g. the increased use of easily [sic] accessible screens such as smartphones and tablets)" (Ghekiere, 2019). Since 2002, the mobile revolution has come, and it's much easier for a young person to sit up with a phone or tablet in their bed.

Technology impacts sleep negatively, and those effects are wide-ranging and powerful. How can parents monitor and regulate technology to improve the family's sleep?

- No *phones in the bedroom*. This is not a solution for everyone. A parent may be on call or in a job in which they need to be near their phone. However, most teens are not on call 24/7 and do not have the same need for a cell phone in their room.
- *Charge the phone in another room*. If a phone is charging in the room, even several feet away, it can still be a distraction with lights and noise.
- *Use sound machines and alarm clocks*. A sound machine can produce white noise, which is the combination of many noises and can mask other sounds. There are some alarm clocks and smartphone devices that can set white noise along with alarms. Try not to use your cell phone for an alarm; just buy a simple alarm clock.
- *Turn off notifications and turn on sleep mode*. Utilize the sleep mode setting on the phone to limit notifications and keep it quiet. Turn off notifications with the possible exception of phone calls. You can also limit phone calls to just a few emergency contacts.
- *Utilize night mode/night shift and dark mode*. Night mode/shift is a setting on the phone that changes the colors of the displayer to warmer tones. Dark mode inverts the color scheme from light backgrounds with dark text, to dark backgrounds with white text. In addition to saving battery life, it can limit the amount of blue light coming through the phone.
- *Use timers and shut-down apps*. There are different apps and timers that parents can set at night. Use parental controls to adjust settings or have your WiFi shut down at night.
- *Have a tech cut-off in the evening*. Try to give at least 30 minutes of no technology before sleep. An hour or even two is better to help your body wind down. Consider setting a charging station that all devices go to at a certain time of day.
- *Read on a book, not a tablet*. The book *Why We Sleep* reports that "compared to reading a printed book, reading on an iPad suppresses melatonin release by over 50 percent at night. Indeed, iPad reading delayed the rise of melatonin by up to

three hours, relative to the natural rise in these same individuals when reading a printed book."

(Walker, 2018)

In addition to reinforcing norms and having family bedtime policies, parents need to model healthy norms for sleep for their children. It's unrealistic to expect children, particularly adolescents, to follow household rules if the parents do not also follow them. Parents should ask themselves questions about their bedtime tech habits:

- When do I put away screens at night?
- Are my devices in my room or on my bed?
- Where do I charge my devices?
- Am I going to bed at a reasonable hour?
- Am I consistent with my sleep schedules?

Mindfulness and Meditation

To be healthy and a positive digital citizen, the skill of self-regulation is vital. Young people must be able to regulate their own screen time use, focus, think before reacting, manage their time, and get adequate sleep. Parents can assist with these skills while they are young, but one day it will ultimately be the responsibility of the child, now young adult, to be able to self-regulate. One skill parents can teach children to assist with self-regulation is mindfulness and meditation. Mindfulness is the practice of paying purposeful and nonjudgmental attention to a person's surroundings and mental state. You accept whatever feelings and sensations you have and let them go.

Mindfulness is a deep and slow thinking state. There is no planning or forecasting with mindfulness, it's just existing. Mindfulness is not encouraged through technology with a multitude of information, pings, buzzing, and more. It's hard to focus and think deeply when there are so many distractions. The American Psychological Association reports research of more than 200 mindfulness studies among healthy people and discovered that "mindfulness-based therapy was especially effective for reducing stress, anxiety and depression" (APA, 2019). Much of the benefit is the ability to help calm down the body's response to stress. When the body is stressed, like with sleep deprivation, it's more susceptible to both physical and mental illness.

Textbox 6.1

In my work with Digital Respons-Ability we incorporate mindfulness instruction in all of our student digital citizenship classes. One concept we teach younger children is the L.A.S.T. technique. It's an acronym to help children calm their brains and get help when confronted by content online that may make them uncomfortable. L.A.S.T. stands for Leave the screen, Ask an adult, Say something, and Think. Leaving the screen allows the child to take a break and calm any emotions they have. The last step, "think," is to help the child evaluate how the content appeared in the first place so it's less likely to happen again. The "think" is also to help them mindfully reflect on their own emotions from the incident.

Mindfulness and Meditation Apps

While it may sound odd, you can fight tech distractions—with more tech. There are many apps, blockers, timers, and other software out there to help your family focus during homework times, stay on task, get to bed, and be digitally healthy. Here are some apps that can help. For more resources see Chapter 8.

- *Forest. Forest* gamifies focus. The user sets goals on how and how long they will use their device. *Forest* plants a tree seed, and the more you keep to those goals, the more your tree will grow. But if you break them, the tree will wither. These are real seeds and real trees, so your digital behavior affects the real world.
- *Headspace.* This popular app has guided meditations, basic mindfulness techniques, and resources and guides to reduce stress and encourage sleep.
- *Moshi: Sleep and Mindfulness.* This mindfulness app is aimed at children who may struggle with bedtimes. It has soothing stories, meditations, lullabies, and ambient noise.
- *Insight Timer.* Rated the top free meditation app in 2020, this app includes mindfulness lessons, videos, music tracks, and thousands of guided meditations.
- *Ten Percent Happier Meditation.* This app provides guided meditations on various topics, stories, inspiration, and other content.

- *Breathe, Think, Do With Sesame.* This app from PBS's *Sesame Street* is aimed at preschoolers. It has character-driven deep breathing exercises and other activities to help young children calm themselves.

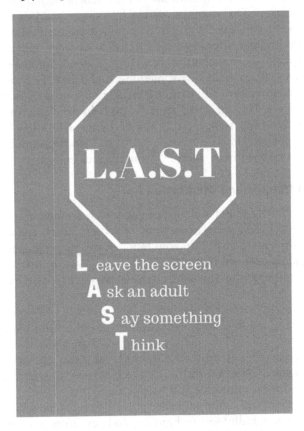

Figure 6.1 The L.A.S.T. Technique Taught to Elementary Students

Strategies and Suggestions for Family Screen Time Issues

Karina Gathu is a working mother of a 3-year-old and expresses her biggest parental concern about technology—screen time:

My biggest concern is just too much screen time. My husband and I both work full time and also my husband just likes TV and screens. He wakes up and turns the TV on. He comes home and turns it on. While I wanted to have limited to no screens for our son, it just wasn't a reality I could implement for a lot of reasons. I don't really have an issue with my three-year-old watching the things he loves— right now it's videos of Hot Wheels and monster trucks on YouTube, I just don't want that to be the only thing. He wakes up and asks for YouTube right away, which I hate. I say no a lot, but yes just as much. Our son is really active and likes to play sports and play, but mostly wants someone to play with him, and so as a parent, sometimes we rely on the screen too much as a babysitter.

(Rogers-Whitehead, 2020, interview with Karina Gathu)

Screen time is a concern for many parents like Karina, although perhaps not as big an issue as some of the media would have people believe. This chapter examined the research behind screen time, which, while more data is needed, shows that screen time is more a symptom of other causes and has smaller effects than we think. However, screen time is something parents should monitor and create healthy family norms around. According to research, parents should be concerned about screen time because of these issues:

- It encourages sedentary behavior, which can affect physical health.
- It affects the amount of sleep.
- It takes children away from other activities/hobbies.
- It distracts from homework, particularly online learning.
- It can limit social time with family and friends.
- The higher the amount of screen time, the higher the risk of encountering cyberbullying or online predators.
- For children with preexisting conditions, like mental illness, screen time can exacerbate those illnesses by isolating the child and fostering social comparison.

It should be noted that screen time can be a hobby and activity for children. An artistic child may create art behind a screen, or an aspiring writer may read other writings for inspiration. In addition, many family and friends are behind a screen and devices can be a tool for connection as well as isolation. Screen time can be a protective factor for some children, and these issues of screen time can be mitigated with regular communication, education, and family strategies for screens.

Some parenting strategies to establish healthy amounts of screen time are included here. Other suggestions for parents can be found in other chapters; for gaming parenting strategies, see Chapter 7.

- *Give choice.* Instead of saying "only 30 minutes to play your game" for older children, consider telling them, "You have three hours of gaming until Saturday. You can choose how you want to spend that time." This encourages time management skills and encourages children to monitor their own usage.
- *Do not count homework or education as screen time.* If your family decides on a set number of hours behind a screen, do not include in that total any learning time.
- *Family time behind screens is different.* Like with homework, families should see time spent together behind screens as positive behaviors, not negative. If you watch a movie or play a game as a family, shift your mindset from "too much screen time" to "We need more family time."
- *Take a break.* When you or your child are sick, you're traveling long distances, it's a snow day, and so on, relax your screen time rules. When the routine is disrupted by closures, sickness, travel, or other factors, the routine of screen time should also change.
- *Monitor mobile devices.* Mobile devices are more isolating; it's why the American Academy of Pediatrics recommends limiting them for children ages 6 and older. When examining screen time, look at TVs and mobile devices differently.
- *Evaluate your own screen time behavior.* Are you setting an example for the family? How do you use screens? If you implement family rules concerning screen time, make sure you follow them as well.

Parents should give themselves a break. A lot of the concerns about screen time don't necessarily have anything to do with technology. Simply being a proactive parent can prevent issues from happening. Michael Robb, Senior Researcher with Common Sense Media, offers this advice to parents:

> One thing I like to say is that even though we don't know the effects of technology we know a lot of things that help kids' development in healthy ways, like being social with friends,

going outside, getting good sleep, playing, having a family dinner. There's lots of good things we can do that don't involve just regulating what they do on screens. If your kid seems to be doing well in all other aspects, they get good grades, they're social, they're sleeping, I think parents don't need to worry about their screen time. Don't add worry when there's no reason to worry.

(Rogers-Whitehead, 2020, interview with Michael Robb)

Summary Points: Screen Time

- Much of the fear about screen time is based on media hyperbole and flaws in screen time research.
- Some flaws in screen time research include utilizing time use studies which do not describe how the screens are used, confusing correlation with causation, conflicting studies and reports, inaccuracies in self-reporting, lack of a common definition of screen time, and bias in researchers and subjects.
- The prevention science framework teaches us that screen time use is a symptom of other causes and can be either a risk factor or a protective factor.
- Online homework can cause stress at home due to lack of digital literacy skills, confusing instruction, multiple logins and software, and unrealistic expectations of educators.
- Screens emit blue light, which can inhibit melatonin production and cause sleep difficulties. The lack of sleep is a risk factor for many physical and emotional problems.
- Mindfulness and meditation are strategies that can help individuals be more emotionally aware of the effects of screens, and help people sleep.

References

Adams, Douglas. *The Salmon of Doubt: Hitchiking the Galaxy One Last Time*. New York: Pocket Books, 2002.
Barrett, Lisa. *How Emotions Are Made: The Secret Life of the Brain*. New York: Mariner Books, 2018.

Coyne, Sarah M., Adam A. Rogers, Jessica D. Zurcher, Laura Stockdale, and Mccall Booth. "Does Time Spent Using Social Media Impact Mental Health?: An Eight Year Longitudinal Study." *Computers in Human Behavior* 104 (2020): 106160. https://doi.org/10.1016/j.chb.2019.106160.

Gathu, Karina. Conversation with the author April 2020.

Ghekiere, A., J. Van Cauwenberg, A. Vandendriessche, et al. "Trends in Sleeping Difficulties among European Adolescents: Are These Associated with Physical Inactivity and Excessive Screen Time?" *International Journal of Public Health* 64 (2019): 487–498. https://doi.org/10.1007/s00038-018-1188-1.

Guerrero, Michelle D., Joel D. Barnes, Jean-Philippe Chaput, and Mark S. Tremblay. "Screen Time and Problem Behaviors in Children: Exploring the Mediating Role of Sleep Duration." *The International Journal of Behavioral Nutrition and Physical Activity*. BioMed Central, November 14, 2019. www.ncbi.nlm.nih.gov/pmc/articles/PMC6854622/.

Keith, Emma. "Norman Parents Express Concerns with School Technology Use at Board Meeting." *Norman Transcript*, January 14, 2020. www.normantranscript.com/news/education/norman-parents-express-concerns-with-school-technology-use-at-board-meeting/article_e3c7c87a-8a9a-5916-b5c7-06e3086c55a2.html.

Lapus, Merve. Conversation with the author April 2020.

"Mindfulness Meditation: A Research-Proven Way to Reduce Stress." American Psychological Association (APA), October 30, 2019. www.apa.org/topics/mindfulness-meditation.

Odgers, Candice L., and Michaeline R. Jensen. "Annual Research Review: Adolescent Mental Health in the Digital Age: Facts, Fears, and Future Directions." *Journal of Child Psychology and Psychiatry* 61, no. 3 (2020): 336–348. https://doi.org/10.1111/jcpp.13190.

O'Keeffe, G.S., and K. Clarke-Pearson. "The Impact of Social Media on Children, Adolescents, and Families." *Pediatrics* 127, no. 4 (2011): 800–804. https://doi.org/10.1542/peds.2011-0054.

Popper, Nathaniel. "Panicking about Your Kids' Phones? New Research Says Don't." *The New York Times*, January 17, 2020. www.nytimes.com/2020/01/17/technology/kids-smartphones-depression.html?algo=identity.

Robb, Michael. Conversation with the author March 2020.

Rogers-Whitehead, Carrie. "5 Tips to Help Your Kid Put Down the Screen and Go to Sleep." *KSL.com*. May 3, 2018. www.ksl.com/article/46313498/5-tips-to-help-your-kid-put-down-the-screen-and-go-to-sleep.

"Sleep for Teenagers." *Sleep Foundation*, June 1, 2020. www.sleepfoundation.org/articles/teens-and-sleep.

Tamminen Lecturer, Jakke. "How a Lack of Sleep Affects Your Brain and Personality." *The Conversation*, September 18, 2018. https://theconversation.com/how-a-lack-of-sleep-affects-your-brain-and-personality-66604.

Truong, Debbie. "More Students Are Learning on Laptops and Tablets in Class: Some Parents Want to Hit the Off Switch." *The Washington*

Post. WP Company, February 1, 2020. www.washingtonpost.com/local/
education/more-students-are-learning-on-laptops-and-tablets-in-class-
some-parents-want-to-hit-the-off-switch/2020/02/01/d53134d0-db1e-
11e9-a688–303693fb4b0b_story.html.

Twenge, Jean. "Have Smartphones Destroyed a Generation?" *The Atlantic*.
Atlantic Media Company, September, 2017. www.theatlantic.com/magazine/
archive/2017/09/has-the-smartphone-destroyed-a-generation/534198/.

Walker, Matthew. *Why We Sleep: The New Science of Sleep and Dreams*.
London: Allan Lane an imprint of Penguin Books, 2018.

Yoo, Seung-Schik, Ninad Gujar, Peter Hu, Ferenc A. Jolesz, and Matthew
P. Walker. "The Human Emotional Brain without Sleep: A Prefrontal
Amygdala Disconnect." *Current Biology* 17, no. 20 (2007). https://doi.
org/10.1016/j.cub.2007.08.007.

Yoon, Sunkyung, Mary Kleinman, Jessica Mertz, and Michael Brannick.
"Is Social Network Site Usage Related to Depression? A Meta-Analysis
of Facebook: Depression Relations." *Journal of Affective Disorders* 248
(2019): 65–72. https://doi.org/10.1016/j.jad.2019.01.026.

Chapter 7

Gaming
A Potential Pitfall or Positive

Joe Ellis, a father of six, described an experience with video games in his family he's never forgotten:

> *Mario Kart* has also played a pretty large role in our family. Last year my wife's brother was moving between two states and had a month that they needed somewhere to live. We had the room in our basement to let his family live for a month, in cramped quarters. Mom, Dad, and four kids moved in to our one-bedroom basement adding to our family of 8. Their kids range from 13 to 6. In what could have been a very taxing month on emotions turned in to a month of cousins vying for *Mario Kart* dominance. Our living room turned in to race central and the memories created will stay with them for a life time.
> (Rogers-Whitehead, 2020, interview with Joe Ellis)

Gaming is part of life for many families and has the power to bring people together such as with Joe's family. Games are in our purses, pockets, and every available screen. As said in the first chapter, "Over half of regular gamers are under 35, with about a third of those under 18" (Gough, 2019). Your children are probably gaming, even if they don't do it regularly. It's hard to find a family that is not touched in some way by the proliferation and growth of gaming. This chapter will debunk myths about gaming, share the pros and cons, and provide families suggestions and ideas for gaming. Gaming can create contention or connection; it can make a basement feel cozy or cramped.

Debunking Myths About Gaming

Chris Ferguson is a professor of psychology and researcher on media, particularly video games. He is the co-author of *Moral Combat:*

Why the War on Violent Video Games is Wrong and has worked for decades debunking myths about video games in the media. In 2019 he published a study in the *Journal of Youth and Adolescence* called "Pathological Gaming in Young Adolescents: A Longitudinal Study Focused on Academic Stress and Self-Control in South Korea."

In South Korea, more than 90% of adolescents play video games. Gaming is also big business in the country, which exported over six billion dollars in games in 2017. South Korea is similar to China, which first started "Internet addiction camps." It has passed legislation regulating video games and has clinics and rehab centers. In 2011 South Korea passed a "Cinderella Law" that required games to have an automatic shutdown for children 15 or younger after midnight. The children quickly found workarounds (Jeong et. al, 2019). According to the South Korean government in 2013, about one in ten South Korean children between the ages of 10 and 19 are "addicted" to the Internet (Kim, 2013). The issue of gaming in South Korea is a controversy and a concern, which is why Ferguson and his co-researchers focused their work there.

Ferguson described this work. "We did release a study with a Korean sample and in this Korean sample, to put it bluntly, it was the parent's fault. Parents were pushing kids to be academically successful so hard and they broke their kids . . . some of these kids developed pathologically [sic] gaming symptoms" (Rogers-Whitehead, 2020, interview with Christopher Ferguson). The gaming was a symptom, not a cause. These teens had risk factors such as authoritarian parents, a culture that pressed for academic success, lack of sleep because of studying, and high amounts of stress. They were particularly at risk for unhealthy digital behaviors because of individual, family, and community risk factors.

"Those parents wanted to say that this was a disease in their kids, but the data showed that it was the parent's fault," said Ferguson. "It's a *your* problem not a *their* problem" (Rogers-Whitehead, 2020, interview with Christopher Ferguson). Parents, educators, and the media like to point the finger at games or their children. Like social media, gaming can be a scapegoat. But also like social media, gaming can make underlying conditions and problems worse.

Ferguson is currently replicating this study with a Singapore sample. He and his co-researchers are finding the same issues. There is more push-back on the concept of "gaming addiction" in recent years in South Korea. As reported in the *Los Angeles Times*, Kim Jung-tae, a professor of game studies and veteran game developer, said the movement against games is a "witch hunt perpetrated by psychiatrists and bureaucrats who stand to profit from funding for research and treatment as well as parents eager to explain away their children's academic failures" (Kim, 2019).

Is Gaming Addiction Real?

Gaming is a hot topic among researchers, therapists, parents, educators, and the media. The World Health Organization (WHO) in 2018 defined gaming disorder in the *International Classification of Diseases, 11th Revision* (ICD-11) (WHO, 2020). The ICD helps identify health trends globally and is "used by medical practitioners around the world to diagnose conditions and by researchers to categorize conditions."

The ICD-11 defines gaming addiction as follows:

> [A] pattern of gaming behavior ("digital-gaming" or "video-gaming") characterized by impaired control over gaming, increasing priority given to gaming over other activities to the extent that gaming takes precedence over other interests and daily activities, and continuing or escalation of gaming despite the occurrence of negative consequences. For gaming disorder to be diagnosed, the behavior pattern must be of sufficient severity to result in significant impairment in personal, family, social, educational, occupational or other important areas of function and would normally have been evident for at least 12 months.
>
> (WHO, 2020)

Unlike the World Health Organization, the American Psychological Association (APA) does not consider internet gaming a mental disorder (APA, 2020). The APA uses the *Diagnostic and Statistical Manual of Mental Disorders* (DSM-5) to make diagnoses and guide research. It does include addictive disorders such as alcohol, opioids, and gambling, but nothing about the Internet and gaming.

Regarding the debate, Professor Ferguson said,

> There is a lot of controversy and mixed opinions. . . . The WHO made an official diagnosis, and a lot of people don't like it. Some people do like it. The group that I belong to which is the media psychology division of the APA got together and wrote a policy statement opposing the WHO so there's a lot of acrimony—there are people that are really angry at each other.
>
> (Rogers-Whitehead, 2020, interview with Christopher Ferguson)

That 2018 policy statement signed by Ferguson, other researchers and professors, and the Psychological Society of Ireland shares concerns about the WHO's decision to include gaming disorders in the ICD-11 (Publisher, 2018). The policy statement includes reasons why they opposed the decision:

> Research on what may loosely be called "video game addiction" has been ongoing for 30 years. Nonetheless, that research has not provided clarity on how to define video game addiction (VGA), what symptoms best diagnose it, how prevalent it is, or whether it truly exists as an independent disorder, or, when it occurs is merely symptomatic of other, underlying mental health diagnoses. Some recent research suggests that the VGA construct lacks clinical utility, with those high in VGA no more likely to experience mental health or physical problems than those low in VGA. . . . Other research has suggested that VGA is unstable, with most of those experiencing high symptoms at one time point seeing them resolved several months later without treatment. . . . Still other research has suggested that symptoms of VGA arise from other mental health disorders, not uniquely from gaming . . . and this is more symptom than disorder.

Ferguson and other researchers do not deny there are issues with gaming. Those issues and potential strategies to solve them will be discussed later in this chapter. They just believe the issue is more complicated than the media and others present it. Ferguson said, "I think that's a nuanced issue. It's not like heroin. There's a lot of rubbish stuff out there like dopamine and variable reinforcement activities . . . literally fishing is a variable reinforcement activity" (Rogers-Whitehead, 2020, interview with Christopher Ferguson).

The panic and fear regarding gaming can be a problem in itself. If a parent shames their child for gaming, or bans it completely, that can cause more issues. "There's a lot of information out there that sounds scarier than it is," said Ferguson. "One to three percent of gamers are maybe seeing some impairment mostly because they have preexisting mental health issues" (Rogers-Whitehead, 2020, interview with Christopher Ferguson). The media psychology division also echoes the concerns about fear in their statement:

> We note that, certainly, some individuals may overdo gaming. However, this is true for a wide range of activities, including

sex, food, work, exercise, shopping, even dance. . . . We can discern no clear reason why video games are being singled out for a disorder rather than a general "behavioral addiction" category if the concern were truly regarding clinical access for those with problem behaviors. Thus, an obsessive focus of the WHO on VGA would appear to us to be a response to moral panic . . . one which in turn is likely to fuel more moral panic, including miscommunications that game playing can be compared to substance abuse.

(Publisher, 2018)

More research is needed on this subject, particularly as technology and games evolve and get into more homes. But what parents should do is look beyond the gaming and the particular games and react with curiosity, not fear.

Textbox 7.1

Gaming is a concern of many parents of children with autism spectrum disorder (ASD). A qualitative study published in 2019 in *Behavioral Sciences* reported what caregivers said about how their children with ASD utilized screens. It found that individuals with ASD were on TVs and video games more compared to their neurotypical peers (Stiller et al., 2019).

Now of course this can be a concern related to physical health and risks for issues regarding online safety. But is it a cause for alarm and panic?

Professor Ferguson said, "A lot of people who have high functioning autism are very uncomfortable in real life and have difficulty making friends. They feel more comfortable with non-face to face communication. They can play what they want to write instead of responding to extemporaneous conversation. What happens to people with autism, they turn to games to get their social needs met. If you take that away you take away their social connections" (Rogers-Whitehead, 2020, interview with Christopher Ferguson).

In a 2018 study published in the *British Journal of Educational Technology*, children with autism played an online game called *Zoo U*. The study "found a significant and positive effect of the game-based learning problem in enhancing the participants' parent and self-reported social skills, functioning and self-confidence" (Ke and Moon, 2018). Video gaming can also encourage development of fine motor skills and collaboration.

Concerns About Gaming

While research suggests that many concerns and fear about gaming is overblown, there are genuine reasons parents and caregivers should monitor and regulate gaming in the home. This section will discuss issues with gaming, but it's important to keep in mind that just as every child is unique, every game is unique. Also, parents should understand that the fears about media have always existed and think back to when they were younger and what their parents said. "There are actually papers in the 1940s in leading scientific journals on radio addiction," said Professor Ferguson. "Then movies, then TV is different than movies. It's always something" (Rogers-Whitehead, 2020, interview with Christopher Ferguson). The "somethings" in this chapter are the mechanics of gaming, microtransactions and loot boxes, violence, gaming culture, and effects on physical health. Perhaps a scientifically reviewed journal article in the 2040s will dismiss some of the research and assertions mentioned here.

Physical Health and Gaming

Rates of obesity in children have doubled over the last thirty years. Obesity, which means the body mass index is at or above the 95th percentile, causes increased risk for diabetes, heart disease, and other preventable illness. The Centers for Disease Control (CDC) estimate that among children and teens between 2 and 19 years old, about 19% are obese ("Childhood Obesity Facts," 2019).

The increase in obesity is cause for alarm for parents and researchers. Since the 1980s there have been reams of research on screen time and obesity. These studies have primarily focused on TV, and more research needs to be conducted on newer media like mobile and online games. However, this lack of research has not stopped the finger of blame from being pointed at video games. In *Moral Combat: Why the War on Violent Video Games is Wrong*, the authors note, "But while modern society as a whole has certainly been criticized by the public and the media for contributing to weight gain, somehow video games in particular are often singled out for an extra share of the blame" (Markey and Ferguson, 2017).

It's clear that obesity is a problem and something parents should be concerned about. But what exactly is the cause of the problem? What is the WHY? Yes, there are links and associations between gaming and obesity, but educators should look closer at the links. Is gaming actually causing obesity?

Examine the changes in society during those thirty years when obesity rates doubled:

- *Our economy has changed.* There are more workers in knowledge-based fields, which are typically sedentary. We move less in our regular jobs.
- *Children's days are more sedentary.* Unlike generations past, children do not contribute to the household, such as working on a farm or tending to younger siblings. Much of their day is sitting. Many schools have cut out recess.
- *Less play time.* For the last fifty years children have had less time to play. Along with this affecting emotional and social development, it means they are moving less (Entin, 2011).
- *More sugar-sweetened beverages.* A 2017 study in the *Journal of Pediatrics* found a connection between TV, gaming, and other screen device use and drinking more sugar-laden beverages. The availability of these beverages and the size of them have also increased (Kenney and Gortmaker, 2017).
- *Fewer vegetables and fruits.* Epidemiologic studies find that "children who consume more screen media also consume fewer fruits and vegetables and more energy-dense snacks." Other studies find that individuals behind screens don't always notice what they're consuming (Robinson et al., 2017).
- *Food advertising.* There is more food advertising directed at young people. Through gaming and other screen use, they can see more options of high-energy foods and beverages.

The authors of *Moral Combat* summarize the issue: "The primary reason for the obesity epidemic is straightforward—we've decreased how much we move around and increased how much we eat" (Markey and Ferguson, 2017). There are associations in gaming related to lack of movement and consuming unhealthy foods and drinks while playing. But those are associations not causes. Unfortunately, the causes are complex and systemic. We cannot point the finger at just one thing, and those things are often out of our control.

But what *is* in a parent's control? The first strategy a parent might implement when they are concerned about gaming and their child's physical health is to cut back or ban the games. That seems like common sense, right? However, research doesn't necessarily support that strategy. A large study in the *International Journal of Obesity* of 44,000 children found that television usage accounted for only about 1% of a child's total weight gain (Braithwaite et al., 2013). There is not a strong relationship between screen time and weight. There are strong relationships between cutting out soda and weight. There are also strong relationships between getting a good night's sleep and weight. If a parent wants to make an impact on their child's physical health, they should not focus too much on their screen use.

If your child, like many others, loves gaming, consider using that existing love to burn more calories. Video games have the potential for increasing activity and decreasing weight loss. Compared to television, video gaming burns more calories (Jamruk, 2019). "Sedentary video game play involves more caloric expenditure than television viewing," according to a 2013 article in *New Directions for Child & Adolescent Development* (Blumberg et al., 2013). The article goes on to summarize new and growing research on "exergames" and mobile games that "have untapped promise to get youth to exercise and even lose weight." They found one powerful way that the games could help with these goals was through social influence. Games that are competitive or played with others and require more movement yield longer-lasting changes (Blumberg et al., 2013).

Some examples of "exergames" that can encourage physical activity include:

- *Pokémon Go*
- *Wii Sports*
- *Wii Fit*
- *Ring Fit*
- *Just Dance*
- *Dance Dance Revolution*
- *GoNoodle Games*
- *Zombies Run!*
- *Sports Party*

- *Beat Saber* (VR)
- *Zumba Fitness*

Game Mechanics

A criticism among parents and gamers is the concept called "grinding." In video games, grinding is performing repetitive tasks for experience points, advantages, unlocking activities, or new characters. A similar term, "farming," is used when players are trying to get loot, whether that be game coins, weapons, or other items. Grinding is a big part of the game in Massively Multiplayer Online Role-Playing Games (MMORPGs). In MMORPGs the development of a character is the primary goal. Some examples of popular MMORPGs are *World of Warcraft* (the most popular game), *Final Fantasy XIV, The Elder Scrolls Online, Runescape, EVE Online,* and *Star Wars: The Old Republic* (Wikipedia, 2020). Every game has its own approach to grinding and some can be more rewarding to players than others. For example, in *Runescape* players can cook items, mine ore, and craft weapons to level. *World of Warcraft* and *Elder Scrolls Online,* in response to some complaints about grinding by players, now have a "rest" feature that can help casual players keep up by providing experience and bonuses over certain time periods, even if the player isn't logged in.

The mechanics of grinding go beyond MMORPGs, however. Developers have found that introducing grinding elements can bring in more money. Free-to-play games that are available to download on mobile devices and/or PC often include lots of grinding. For example, in *Pokémon Go* you can walk and take the time to get Poké Balls and other items through Poké Stops or battles, or you can simply use real money to purchase them and bypass the work. *Fortnite: Battle Royale* has used grinding mechanics to huge financial returns. You can farm V-bucks, the game's currency, which allows you to get weapons and more, or you can simply buy them.

Grinding can cost money and time. It can take a child away from doing their homework or other necessary tasks. It can pull someone away from friends in the quest for the best weapon or the next level. It can encourage stress or compulsions in children who are particularly prone to anxiety or the desire to succeed. Another word for "grinding" is "treadmilling." Gamers can feel they are on a constant treadmill with no end in sight.

However, some gamers embrace grinding and find it provides satisfaction. They may feel a sense of accomplishment; or as Julie Muncy writes in *WIRED*, grinding helped her through her depression. She plays multiplayer online games (MMOs) in the summer when her seasonal depression hits (Muncy, 2019):

> These days I have another theory about why myself and others I know play MMOs in the summer. Maybe it's because everyone's as depressed as I am. And grinding, in its imitation of forward movement, is catnip to a mind stuck in neutral. Videogames have never cured my depression, and are generally not the answer to mental illness, but grinding makes it easier for me to think. The constant forward movement, not demanding or exciting but still, inexorably, movement, has an effect on me. It clears out the cobwebs, depression lays down, making my mind feel a little quicker, a little more awake. I can think about things better when I'm grinding. Playing games like this can help my mood. Like ersatz mental calisthenics. If nothing else, it's better than staring at the walls. Even if, really, all I'm staring at is an imaginary Mars.

Grinding is controversial and parents should be aware that many popular games include this mechanic. However, depending on the motivation and the child, the gamer may find stress or solace.

Microtransactions and Loot Boxes

In 2019 a free game made over 1.8 billion dollars (Gonzalez, 2020). This sentence makes no sense, unless you understand the game mechanics and economics of microtransactions. The billion-plus-dollar game is *Fortnite*, which as discussed in Chapter 4 is declining in revenue, but still has many players. *Fortnite* makes most of its money not from the player buying the game, but from small purchases through V-bucks (Fortnite's in-game currency). Players spend their V-bucks on in-game cosmetics such as new outfits, moves, customizations of characters, or items. And many of these players are children buying game content with their parent's credit card.

For children, particularly in the tween years, being able to customize their character is important to them. Parents may not get the appeal, but for young people, how their avatar is dressed can be just as important as how *they* are dressed. Games can be how they interact with their friends, and how they express their identity. You can see this in games like Nintendo's *Animal Crossing*, wherein players can decorate the inside and outside of their home.

These purchases on apps and games are called microtransactions, because they are typically very small, like a dollar or two. But those dollars can add up quickly—as evidenced by games like *Fortnite*. A type of microtransaction is a loot box. Loot boxes are digital treasure chests, also called loot crates. Sometimes a player gets a loot box through game play, other times by paying a fee (Rogers-Whitehead, 2019). There are three different types or categories of loot boxes.

In the late 2010s loot boxes became controversial, particularly with the game *Star Wars Battlefront*. The game increased the cost of loot boxes and put valuable characters and game content inside, so those who spent additional money on the game had a greater advantage. Sometimes gamers will know what's in a loot box before purchase; other times they will not. In *Star Wars Battlefront* they did not always know what was in the box and could end up spending more money on many boxes to get the right character or item. Players pushed back on EA, the game's manufacturer, causing its stock to drop (Rogers-Whitehead, 2019).

Another type of controversial loot box is one which requires players to pay money to be more successful. It's not necessarily a "box" but some kind of item or mechanic that the player is all but forced to purchase. It can be found in certain types of collectible card games, like *Magic the Gathering*. Players will spend more money on having specific powerful or rare cards. This type of loot box can also be seen in other games like *Call of Duty* wherein certain items are restricted until the player has paid for them.

The last category of loot boxes can be found in games like *Fortnite* and *Overwatch*. It's a cosmetic loot box. Paying for a specific customized "skin" in one of those games will not give you an inherent advantage in game play. This type of loot box has had less push back, because it's not a surprise, or like a slot machine. Players know what they're getting, and it doesn't give them an advantage in game play.

A criticism of loot boxes is that they can encourage compulsive gambling. The Federal Trade Commission (FTC) started investigating loot boxes in late 2018. Other governments have looked into the practice and in 2018 Belgium ruled that loot boxes were a form of gambling (Rogers-Whitehead, 2018). The FTC had a workshop in fall 2019 called Inside the Game: Unlocking the Consumer Issues Surrounding Loot Boxes. One of the panelists was Jeff Haynes, who is a senior editor of video games with Common Sense Media. He describes the controversy with loot boxes:

> These are slot machine style mechanics, where paying extra possibly gives players more chances to earn higher rewards. But the developers control both the odds as well as the payout for these items. That tempts players into spending more money for additional chances to win rarer items, which could easily trigger people that have compulsive gambling urges.
>
> ("Inside the Game: Unlocking the Consumer Issues Surrounding Loot Boxes," 2019)

Children's brains are still developing, and they have less ability to self-regulate. It's hard enough for an adult to step away from those mechanics; it's even more difficult for a young person. Haynes goes onto add,

> Even people with restraint can find themselves in fiscal trouble thanks to a separate issue tied innately to loot boxes, which is that of microtransactions. It's important to note that while all loot boxes are microtransactions, not all microtransactions are loot boxes. But consumers that don't pay attention to how much they spend on these smaller purchases can quickly and surprisingly charge hundreds or even thousands of dollars on digital items.
>
> ("Inside the Game: Unlocking the Consumer Issues Surrounding Loot Boxes," 2019)

Like with social media and other technology, it's important to note that loot boxes do not *cause* gambling. Professor Christopher Ferguson said,

> What we find from loot boxes, and I'm referring to other people's work on this—is that all we can really see at the moment is that people who already have problematic gambling habits tend to spend more on loot boxes than non-problematic gamblers. There is no evidence that loot boxes cause any problematic gamblers.
>
> (Rogers-Whitehead, 2020, interview with Christopher Ferguson)

He goes onto question the need for governments to be involved in regulation. "Is that something the federal government should be involved in? Most countries haven't banned it, but Belgium did. There's legislation in the U.S. that hasn't gone anywhere else."

Game manufacturers and others have defended the practice of microtransactions in terms of cost. One of the panels had the lawyer Sean Kane, who represents more than 100 video game companies:

> Games have really changed over the last 15 or 20 years. Really, these things were much more simplistic, they were linear. Now they're open worlds. . . . But with that, the cost of games has skyrocketed. Over the last 15 years, your average AAA game, the cost has risen from, say, maybe $20 to $30 million to over $100 million, and in some cases, over $200 million. Because the cost of developing a game with hundreds if not thousands of hours of play, and then marketing that game is immense.
> ("Inside the Game: Unlocking the Consumer Issues Surrounding Loot Boxes," 2019)

Kane describes how the price of games has not changed in the last ten to fifteen years, but the cost has gone up, "which is why microtransactions populated in the industry quite a lot." While loot boxes and microtransactions are controversial, Kane and others argue that they are part of the price to pay lower costs of games. "If you are going to charge the actual cost of development, that number might be more like $300 to $500 a game" instead of the average cost of sixty dollars ("Inside the Game: Unlocking the Consumer Issues Surrounding Loot Boxes," 2019).

With the cost and competitiveness in the gaming industry, we should not expect microtransactions and loot boxes to go away. They may shift and change on how they are implemented, but developers, particularly those with free-to-play games, rely on them.

Parents should have conversations about "freemium" or "free-to-play" games and put limits on how much should be spent. Young children in particular may struggle to understand how the game's mechanics work and that it's not free. Older children may not understand how they are being marketed to by large corporations. For all ages, parents should encourage children to earn money for these in-game purchases and have the children distinguish *needs* and *wants* in their gaming.

Other ways parents can limit in-game purchases include the following:

- Create passkeys to prevent unauthorized purchases.
- Create separate child accounts.
- Enable restrictions on iPhones and disallow in-app purchases on games like *Fortnite* or others.
- Use Google Play's function that allows you to require a password or authentication for purchases. The Google Play store automatically requires authentication for purchases of apps or games for ages 12 and younger.
- Sign out of consoles and accounts if you are sharing them with your child. That can prevent them from logging into your account, which may be linked to a credit card.
- Do not put any credit card information on children's accounts. Buy them a gift card instead if they want to buy things.

Violence in Video Games

As long as there have been video games, there have been fears and panic about the violence in them. In the research-based nonfiction title *Moral Combat: Why the War on Violent Video Games is Wrong*, the authors describe the first outcry in video games—with the 1975 arcade game *Death Race*. This simple game, with only white and black colors and lines and dots, had characters run over stick figures to get points and tinny screams. Dr. Gerald Driessen, who was with the National Safety Council, "became one of the first psychologists to publicly propose a link between violent video games and real-life violence when he suggested that the interactive nature of the game might cause a small proportion of the population to become violent when they got behind the wheels of real cars." Since *Death Race* there have been many more car games with running down pedestrians, most notably *Grand Theft Auto*. But Driessen's prediction of more pedestrians being killed has not come to pass (Markey and Ferguson, 2017).

Along with other panics and concerns about elements of video games—*They cause school shootings! They make children fat!*—the research does not suggest any links. However, that has still not stopped concerns and legislation. In 2005, then-Senator Hillary Clinton tried to put more federal enforcement behind the Entertainment Software Ratings Board. After the Sandy Hook shootings in 2012, President Barack Obama asked for the CDC to investigate the effects of violent video games (Markey and Ferguson, 2017). The effects of these panics are also found at local and family levels—*Games are banned! Children are shamed!*

The book *Moral Combat* goes on to describe a reason for these panics:

> Very often when a new form of media or technology is released, society goes through a period of moral panic in which this media or technology is blamed for any number of social kills, whether real or merely perceived. These panics can be explained in large part by generation gaps in adopting new technology or media. The young are far more proficient at adapting to innovation than are the old. This can create a perception among older adults that they are losing control of the culture they helped shape.
>
> (Markey and Ferguson, 2017)

There is more to the fears beyond panic; a body of questionable research, media articles, think tanks and politicians, and more have amassed since the first "violent" video game: *Death Race*. In 1986 two researchers published their findings on the Atari 2600 video game *Missile Command* and wrote in their article for the *Journal of Applied Social Psychology* that the game had "measurable consequences" for aggression in the child subjects (Cooper and Mackie, 1986). There are issues with this and subsequent studies on aggression. First, they are self-reported by young people. In addition, they also involve responding to questions/statements like, "I feel unsociable," "I feel willful," or "The person running the study was not very courteous," that are not exactly related to aggression (Cooper and Mackie, 1986). There are also issues with research on the subjectivity not just of self-reporting, but also of what a "violent video game" actually is. *Missile Command* had no blood, no people; it was a rocket shooting black-and-white pixels in space. Another issue with these studies of aggression is that the feelings of frustration and aggression are similar. A gamer playing a difficult level who loses or gets stuck may report negative feelings, but they are not about a desire to be violent, or anger, but frustration of where they are in the game. Finally, it's also good to keep in mind there is a difference between attitudes towards violence and actual behaviors. Just because someone has an unfriendly thought while playing a video game does not mean they will actually go out and perpetrate violence.

There were no follow-up studies or research to the 1986 journal article until the Columbine shootings in 1999. Then there was an explosion of research and media attention. Parents were scared.

Students were scared. They wanted answers. The American Psychological Association (APA) made a policy statement in 2005 that made several statements about video games including:

> **WHEREAS** comprehensive analysis of violent interactive video game research suggests such exposure a.) increases aggressive behavior, b.) increases aggressive thoughts, c.) increases angry feelings, d.) decreases helpful behavior, and, e.) increases physiological arousal.
>
> (APA, 2005)

However, due to the lack of research, the APA has softened and revised its statements. In a press release sent out in Spring 2020, the APA stated, "There is insufficient scientific evidence to support a causal link between violent video games and violent behavior, according to an updated resolution adopted by the American Psychological Association" (APA, 2020). A task force was asked to review its 2015 statement, which reaffirmed the 2005 statement. The APA is now more cautious about claims, writing in their press release, "Violence is a complex social problem that likely stems from many factors. . . . [A]ttributing violence to video gaming is not scientifically sound and draws attention away from other factors, such as a history of violence, which we know from the research is a major predictor of future violence" (APA, 2020).

There is an increasing amount of research pushing back against the narrative begun in the 1980s that video games cause violence. Professor Ferguson said:

> I think that is dying slowly and people are getting tired. It's become increasingly politically polarized. Twenty years ago, liberal and conservatives were jumping on that bandwagon. It really has become a right versus left issue. Largely the idea that video games are related to any public health level of violence or aggression or bullying is a dead issue. . . . It is also risky to make a conclusive statement, but I think culturally it's on its way out.
>
> (Rogers-Whitehead, 2020, interview with Christopher Ferguson)

Part of the reason that moral panic has decreased is that demographics have changed. The children who were told in the 1980s and 1990s that video games they played were the source of so much violence realized that wasn't true. Now those parents are having children, and video games are not such a new form of media.

Parents and caregivers should feel less guilt about certain video games causing more violence or aggression. But they also should follow Entertainment Software Ratings Board (ESRB) ratings and have their children participate in age-appropriate games. Just as most parents would not take an 8-year-old to an R-rated movie they should also avoid Mature-rated games for that age. For a young child, there are many other educational or social games they can play with more benefits than a more violent game like *Grand Theft Auto*. Parents should not necessarily avoid violent or more mature games because of content, but simply because there are many other social, family-friendly, and educational games out there. There is far more than the Atari 2600 nowadays, and families have a bounty of games to choose from. Some of those games will be listed later in this chapter.

Gaming Culture

When you play a game, you're not just playing a game, you're participating in a new culture. This culture has different terms for things ("pwn," "crit," "adds," etc.). Gaming culture has different rules and norms. Some cultures are friendly and welcoming; others are more competitive and can be hostile. When a child plays with gamers from around the world, there is sure to be cross-cultural conflict.

The Cyberbullying Research Center surveyed 1,500 12- to 17-year-olds about gaming and bullying. In their results they found that "students who self-identified as 'gamers' were significantly more likely to have said that they bullied or cyberbullied others during the previous 30 days." They also discovered that "gamers were also more likely than non-gamers to be the victim of bullying at school (40.7% compared to 27.2%) and bullying online (25.9% compared to 15.7%)." So, on its face there seems to be a connection between gaming and bullying (Patchin, 2018).

However, the researchers dived deeper into that connection and controlled for the effects of age, race, and sex and found only a 5% variation between those who cyberbullied. The reasons gamers cyberbullied include:

• *Type of game.* Multiplayer online battles and first-person shooter games had a greater connection to cyberbullying than other types of games.

- *Hours a week played.* Students who played less than two hours a day were far less likely than those who played more to have cyberbullied others.

(Patchin, 2018)

It makes sense that the more a player plays a game, the more opportunity they have to bully others, or be bullied themselves. Games like battles and shooting games are more competitive and have been linked to more self-reports of aggressive (or frustrating) feelings.

When looking at the subject of cyberbullying and gaming, parents should also know more about gaming culture, specifically trolling. What parents and educators define as "cyberbullying" may be actually trolling.

What is the difference between cyberbullying and trolling? This answer can be subjective based on the person and the platform. In gaming culture, trolling can be part of initiation. A "n00b" or "newb" is a new player to the game and others may troll that player until they prove their mettle. Trolls may also target new members of online communities like Discord. But in this type of initiation trolling, one person is not particularly singled out. It's not as personal as cyberbullying.

Textbox 7.2

Many cases of cyberbullying and trolling happen on Discord. This free chat platform was initially designed for gamers and replaced earlier chat services like TeamSpeak. Discord was publicly released in 2015 and has grown rapidly ever since, boasting over 250 million users in 2019 (Rogers-Whitehead, 2018).

On Discord gamers can voice, video, or text chat as well as share screens. It is similar to Slack with different channels on various topics, far beyond games. Discord has received pushback and criticism for its use by the alt-right and other hate groups. It was found that the 2017 Unite the Right rally was planned and organized through Discord. Other channels can have pornography and are known for sharing revenge porn.

Users have to look for, find, and often be accepted into the channels which have adult content. They are not likely to

> stumble upon them, but parents should make sure that controls are set. Discord offers different parental controls such as blocking users from direct messages, limiting what "friends" can add you, and filtering images that may be explicit.

Some trolls, particularly in old-school gaming culture, see trolling as an art. It's a way to make others laugh, provide social commentary, push back at authority, and pass the time. There's a catchphrase and meme, "I did it for the lulz," which means someone posted offensive or hyperbolic comments for the laughs or controversy. Sometimes these posts are simply humorous, but other times they reference topics like suicide, the Holocaust, rape, and more.

A skilled troll doesn't have a particular target; they set a trap. This trap may be a controversial post or comment intended to rile someone up. Trolls want others to be offended or angry. They want responses. They sometimes revel in being banned from sites. When dealing with trolls, the best thing to do is ignore them. They set a trap and wait; they typically won't chase victims.

Unlike a troll, a bully will follow someone around the Internet. They may try to dox their victims and reveal their identities. A bully will try to harass victims on multiple platforms and find out their personal information. A troll may do it for the "lulz" but a bully does it because of rejection, anger, and specific feelings towards their victim as an individual.

This is not to dismiss the real damage a troll can do, but parents and students need to know to handle a troll differently than a bully. In a situation of bullying in a game, young people should report it to the moderators, block the user, or in some situations stop playing. With a troll, they should ignore it and understand that while it may be offensive, it was not a direct attack against them.

This section only talked about some of the negatives of gaming culture, but there are many positives. Justin Hakason, a dad of three boys, describes his experience gaming:

> Gaming has been a part of my life since I was very young. My best friend had an Atari 2600 that we would play with. My parents bought us the original NES when it came out. I also played games with friends in the computer lab at school. Those

friends are still in my circle of friends today. . . . Games have been a big part of my life.

(Rogers-Whitehead, 2020, interview with Justin Hakason)

In gaming culture, players can find friends or frustration, community or contention, just like real life.

Benefits of Gaming

Justin Hakason wished non-gamers knew that playing games is better than watching TV. He said, "My philosophy is I'd much rather have my boys playing games than watching TV. Games provide so much more value. Our TV watching is deliberate, meaning no channel flipping, and only done together as a family. But the kids can play whatever games they want on their own" (Rogers-Whitehead, 2020, interview with Justin Hakason).

Television has been central to American families since the 1950s. While the amount of television American adults view has dropped since 2014 with the proliferation of different screens, it's still a large part of people's routines. Statistica estimates television viewing for adults to be about three and half hours each day in 2020 (Watson, 2019). While there has always been criticism of television since the technology was created, the newer technology of gaming seems to get parents' and the media's attention.

Maybe we should look at that differently. Perhaps we should spend less time concerned about gaming than about other types of screens or activities. Gaming offers benefits that other digital platforms do not. Some of those benefits, like physical activity and connection, were discussed earlier. But there are more benefits, and it's a growing area of research. The authors of *Moral Combat* write that there's a younger generation of researchers who "understand both how games work and how they fit into modern culture. These scholars are changing the nature of the field" (Markey and Ferguson, 2017). Like the field of video game research, parents, caregivers, and educators should shift their perceptions of video gaming.

Education Through Gaming

"My second oldest son learned how to study for tests and do research in school by playing *Terraria* when he was 14," said Joe, father of six. The game *Terraria* is a sandbox game out since 2011 that allows exploration, building, and combat in a 2D world. "*Terraria* has a very in-depth crafting system that requires lots of knowledge to be able to make certain items," Joe goes on to say. "He had to use research skills on the Internet and take notes to figure out what items he would need to finish off whatever item he was crafting. He has commented to me that those skills helped him greatly when he had a research paper to write his junior year in high school" (Rogers-Whitehead, 2020, interview with Joe Ellis.

One way to think about the benefits of video games is through the concept of affinity spaces, as described by Dylan Arena in the journal *Theory into Practice* as the "network of social interactions that arise spontaneously around a good game" (Arena, 2015). For example, Joe's son was inspired by his interest in *Terraria*'s affinity space to learn more. Arena goes on to say:

> A game's affinity space where players reflect on their experiences in the game; wrestle with concepts that they don't fully understand, such as strategies for overcoming a particular obstacle in the game; venture opinions about what might be changed to improve the game experience; serve as peer mentors for newer players; and often move from more peripheral to more central participation in what researchers have called a community of practice.
>
> (Arena, 2015)

These affinity spaces provide both educators and parents opportunities for education. It's easier to engage with students by tapping into their existing interests. Gaming is so popular among students that there are entire ecosystems of knowledge and context that educators can draw from.

Games can also encourage literacy. The MMORPG *World of Warcraft* has a massive affinity space. In a study of middle- and high-school-aged boys with lower-than-normal reading scores, the game *World of Warcraft* helped boost comprehension levels. "The drastic difference in comprehension was driven by a single factor: self-correction rates. In other words, when the boys were reading something they were interested in, they tried harder and reread as necessary to make sure they understood" (Blumberg et al., 2013).

In addition, the visuals paired with the text in gaming can help non-native speakers to better learn a new language. Richard

Mayer's book *Multimedia Learning* discusses the multimedia principle that "people learn better from words and pictures than from words alone" (Mayer, 2001). This finding has been replicated in other research. By having speech bubbles, selecting actions, creating characters, navigating maps, and more, students can better understand new and complex concepts in their own or other languages.

There are also educational games that will be discussed more in Chapter 8. But even games that do not have specific educational components can help students write, read, comprehend, and inspire them to learn.

Lessons Through Gaming

Gaming can also provide a different type of education, one of soft skill. Justin Hakason describes some of those benefits with his three children. "They get a great sense of accomplishment when they beat a level or a game, especially if they can do it before their dad!" While difficult levels can sometimes cause frustration, which can shift to aggression, they can also provide a sense of mastery and purpose.

"Games encourage their creativity," describes Hakason. He sees this creativity both in games and without them. His children love the sandbox building game *Minecraft*. "They plan things out on paper that they want to do in a game or spend time drawing characters and coming up with names for those that may not have them" (Rogers-Whitehead, 2020, interview with Justin Hakason).

Another benefit of games is empathy. They are exposed to different thoughts, ideas, and experiences. They enter other countries, times in history, and worlds. Like books, games can allow the participant a peek into another person's experiences.

Textbox 7.3

Virtual reality (VR) technology has improved in recent years, bringing more players into these immersive worlds. In Spring 2020 the first full-length VR game came out, *Half-Life: Alyx*. After over three years in development and with the largest team in the game manufacturer, Valve's, history, the game has received high praise from those who see it changing the VR game industry.

These immersive games may make parents fearful, particularly since they can be used to consume VR pornography. However, the user base is still small because the equipment and tools needed come at a high cost. The ability for VR games to suck in the user is both a feature and, to others, a bug. Depending on the use of VR they can provide benefits and learning to young people.

Professor Jeremy Bailenson with Stanford studied the effects of people who went through a VR experience called "Becoming Homeless" to see how empathy levels were impacted. In the game, participants experienced the stresses of living on the street. The study found that users who played the VR experience had more "enduring positive attitudes" towards the homeless than those who read narratives and stories about those on the street (Stanford, 2018). VR, like all technology, is a tool that can be used for benefits or detriments, empathy or entertainment.

Games give children a safe place to exercise their autonomy. During the day kids are told where to go, what to eat, what to wear, what to learn, when to go to bed, and much more. A game can be a place where they are in charge. *They* make the decisions. They find that there are consequences of choices. They can learn through losing a boss fight that they have to better prepare and work to be competitive. Children may learn that they have to cooperate with their team or guild to complete the quest and cannot do it on their own.

Unlike television, games require active participation. One cannot sit and passively observe a game. Players must make decisions, practice, work hard, read, talk, strategize, and much more.

Parenting Strategies and Norms for Gaming

Rules are direct and clear cut, and can bring comfort to parents navigating technology. There are rules that are advised in this book, but much of the time the words "norms" and "strategies" are considered. If a family creates positive norms for technology in their home, there is less of a need for rules. Since gaming has clear benefits and not-so-clear detriments, an approach to digital parenting around games should focus on healthy norms with strategies to deal with issues that may arise.

Father of six Joe Ellis does not have gaming rules. "We don't really have rules about gaming in our house, but our kids also don't abuse our trust. They've grown up knowing that game systems are available for them to use. We've yet to come across a reason to enforce strict rules on gaming. Phones on the other hand are turned it at 9pm to a charging station, where they stay until 8am the next day" (Rogers-Whitehead, 2020, interview with Joe Ellis).

In Ellis's home there are positive norms for gaming. "Every January our family goes skiing for a week, and in August we spend a week hiking and swimming," Ellis said. "Both of these family vacations are glued together with gaming. The part that everyone looks forward to is sitting around the table at night playing a board game or getting out one of the game systems and playing couch co-op games" (Rogers-Whitehead, 2020, interview with Joe Ellis). Gaming doesn't have to be bound by strict rules in Ellis's home because it's integrated as a normal part of family time. Gaming isn't the exception or a privilege or a special treat, it's just part of growing up. Games are not taboo or accompanied with lectures or negativity in the home. With no taboos, there's no reason for the children to hide their game play or feel shame or guilt that they are playing.

When developing parenting strategies for gaming, use the three Cs: child, content, context. Look at what your child is interested in, examine the game, its rating, and its content, and consider when and how long they would be engaged in the game. In Chapter 3 the three Cs were discussed for a television show. Let's look at them for a game and a hypothetical tween:

> Sophia is a 12-year-old who got her first phone a couple of months ago. She mainly uses it to talk with her friends and watch videos on YouTube. Sometimes she sneaks her phone into her bedroom late and her parent worries she's getting too little sleep. Recently, Sophia's been asking about a new mobile game her friends are playing: a simulation game on their phones, *Stardew Valley*. In the game players grow and harvest crops as they build a farming enterprise. This game can be played solo or multi-player. The hypothetical tween Sophia's situation can be evaluated using the Three Cs in Table 7.1.

Table 7.1 Using the Three Cs to Evaluate a Game

Three Cs	Questions to Ask	Good for Sophia?
Child	Will *Stardew Valley* keep Sophia's interest? Can she play with her friends?	Sophia loves talking to her friends, and this is another way they can talk together. Even if she isn't interested in farming, the social component will appeal to her.
Content	What is *Stardew Valley* about? Does it cost money or have in-game purchases?	There appears to be no concern about violence/sex in the game. However, it does cost money to play and has microtransactions.
Context	When would Sophia play *Stardew Valley*? Will it keep her up at night?	This simulation game never ends and playing until too late at night could be a concern. Also, the game will follow her since it's on mobile. Sophia's parent needs to have conversations about sleep and money with her.

Part of the strategy should be looking at reviews and the ESRB, the electronic ratings review board. Founded in 1994, the ESRB has ratings from "Early Childhood" to "Adults Only." In 2018, in response from legislative pressure regarding loot boxes, the ESRB also notes any "interactive elements" (ESRB, 2020). Those elements can include "In-Game Purchases" and "Users Interact" which means that players can share content on social media and interact with other players. Another "interactive element" is "Unrestricted Internet" which means that the game can provide access to the Internet through a browser, search engine, or other means (ESRB, 2020). Parents should not just look at the rating, but what "interactive elements" are included in the game.

"I check ESRB ratings to make sure what they play is appropriate," said Hakason, a dad of an 11-year-old and twin 9-year-olds. "At this point they can play E10-rated games and below. If they play a Teen-rated game, it's one I'm familiar with and have decided is appropriate" (Rogers-Whitehead, 2020, interview with Justin Hakason). More information about the ESRB and ratings will be shared in Chapter 8.

Questions to Ask When Finding Family-Friendly Games

"I don't think it's right for parents to *not* take a role in their kids gaming habits and what games they play," said Ellis. I think the biggest thing would be figuring out what games are suitable for your child to be exposed to and monitoring that exposure. The easiest way to do this is to simply play the games with them; however I know that's not realistic for everyone" (Rogers-Whitehead, 2020, interview with Joe Ellis).

If you aren't a gamer or familiar with the game, here are some questions to ask when determining what game is right for your child and your family:

- What's the ESRB rating?
- Does my child have time to play this game?
- Why does my child want to play this game? What are their reasons?
- Does it have microtransactions? If so, can I turn off purchases?
- Is this a game my child will play on mobile? Or another device?
- Does the game have access to the Internet?
- Is there grinding in this game? What are the game mechanics?
- Is this game sedentary or does it have movement?
- Can this game be played as a family? Or is it a solo game?
- Does this game appeal to my child's interest?
- Will my child be talking with others through the game?
- How long is the game? Does it have an end?

When asking these questions, make sure you aren't imposing values, but reinforcing the positive norms in your home. Is gaming in the home actually a problem? Or is it just a problem for you? "There is sort of a sense that my kid isn't doing what I want them to do and that's part of the problem that they're unhappy or dysfunctional," said Professor Ferguson. If you want your child to play a sport, and they're playing a game, is that a problem? Perhaps you want them to play a sport because you enjoyed sports as a kid. Perhaps you want them to play a sport because you want them to be more active. Examine your own reasons for your values about gaming. Ferguson goes on to say, "If your goal is only to reduce their technology use you may be taking away a coping mechanism from them, not replacing it. It should also be part of a larger plan of understanding WHY they use technology in the first place and what it can be replaced with if that's something the person who wants to replace it with" (Rogers-Whitehead, 2020, interview with Christopher Ferguson).

Summary Points: Gaming

- There are myths about gaming, such as that it encourages school shootings and violence, but there is no long-term evidence that gaming can cause violence.
- Gaming, like other screen time, is a symptom of other behaviors, not necessarily a cause.
- There is controversy on the diagnosis of gaming addiction. The World Health Organization uses that definition, but the American Psychological Association does not. Researchers and psychologists question whether gaming addiction actually exists as an independent gaming behavioral disorder or is a symptom of something else.
- Concerns about gaming include lack of physical activity, mechanics such as "grinding" and repeating certain actions, microtransactions and in-game purchases, and toxic gaming culture.
- Benefits of gaming include friendships and positive social connections, education, and developing SEL skills. The benefits of gaming are a new and growing area of research.
- Games are rated through the Entertainment Software Rating Board (ESRB) and parents can read ratings to find out if there are in-game purchases and other specific gaming elements.

References

"APA Reaffirms Position on Violent Video Games and Violent Behavior." *American Psychological Association.* www.apa.org/news/press/releases/2020/03/violent-video-games-behavior (Accessed April 28, 2020).

Arena, D. "Video Games as Tillers of Soil." *Theory Into Practice* 54, no. 2 (2015): 94–100. https://doi.org/10.1080/00405841.2015.1010843.

Blumberg, Fran C., Elizabeth A. Altschuler, Debby E. Almonte, and Maxwell I. Mileaf. "The Impact of Recreational Video Game Play on Children's and Adolescents' Cognition." *New Directions for Child and Adolescent Development* 2013, no. 139 (2013): 41–50. https://doi.org/10.1002/cad.20030.

Braithwaite, Irene, Alistair W. Stewart, Robert J. Hancox, Richard Beasley, Rinki Murphy, and Edwin A. Mitchell. "The Worldwide Association between Television Viewing and Obesity in Children and Adolescents: Cross Sectional Study." *PLoS One* 8, no. 9 (2013): 1–8. doi:10.1371/journal.pone.0074263.

"Childhood Obesity Facts." *Centers for Disease Control and Prevention*, June 24, 2019. www.cdc.gov/obesity/data/childhood.html.

Cooper, J. and D. Mackie. "Video Games and Aggression in Children." *Journal of Applied Social Psychology* 16 (1986): 726–744.

Ellis, Joe. Conversation with the author May 2020.

Entin, Esther. "All Work and No Play: Why Your Kids Are More Anxious . . ." *The Atlantic*, October 21, 2011. www.theatlantic.com/health/archive/2011/10/all-work-and-no-play-why-your-kids-are-more-anxious-depressed/246422/.

Ferguson, Christopher. Conversation with the author March 2020.

"Gaming Disorder." *World Health Organization*. www.who.int/news-room/q-a-detail/gaming-disorder (Accessed April 21, 2020).

Gonzalez, Oscar. "Fortnite Made $1.8 Billion Last Year, But It's Still a Game in Decline." *CNET*, February 22, 2020. www.cnet.com/news/fortnite-made-1-8-billion-last-year-but-its-still-a-game-in-decline/.

Gough, Christina. "U.S. Average Age of Video Gamers 2019." *Statista*, September 18, 2019. www.statista.com/statistics/189582/age-of-us-video-game-players-since-2010/.

Hakason, Justin. Conversation with the author May 2020.

"Home." *ESRB Ratings*. www.esrb.org/ (Accessed April 28, 2020).

"Inside the Game: Unlocking the Consumer Issues Surrounding Loot Boxes." *Federal Trade Commission*, September 24, 2019. www.ftc.gov/news-events/events-calendar/inside-game-unlocking-consumer-issues-surrounding-loot-boxes.

Jamruk, K. "The Weight Game: Fighting Childhood Obesity with Childhood Video Technology." *Journal of Legal Medicine* 37, no. 1/2 (2017): 175–194. https://doi.org/10.1080/01947648.2017.1303409.

Jeong, E.J., C.J. Ferguson, and S.J. Lee. "Pathological Gaming in Young Adolescents: A Longitudinal Study Focused on Academic Stress and Self-Control in South Korea." *Journal of Youth and Adolescence* 48, no. 12 (2019): 2333–2342.

Ke, Fengfeng, and Jewoong Moon. "Virtual Collaborative Gaming as Social Skills Training for High-Functioning Autistic Children." *British Journal of Educational Technology* 49, no. 4 (2018): 728–741. https://doi.org/10.1111/bjet.12626. Wikipedia. "Half Life Alyx" (Accessed April 21, 2020).

Kenney, Erica L., and Steven L. Gortmaker. "United States Adolescents' Television, Computer, Videogame, Smartphone, and Tablet Use: Associations with Sugary Drinks, Sleep, Physical Activity, and Obesity." *The Journal of Pediatrics* 182 (2017): 144–149. https://doi.org/10.1016/j.jpeds.2016.11.015.

Kim, Daum. "Horses to the Rescue of Korea's Internet-Addicted Teens." *Reuters*, January 9, 2013. www.reuters.com/article/us-korea-internet-horses/horses-to-the-rescue-of-koreas-internet-addicted-teens-idUSBRE9080 3020130109.

Kim, Victoria. "He Played for 72 Hours Straight: South Korea Wrestles with Video Game Addiction." *Los Angeles Times*, October 17, 2019. www.latimes.com/world-nation/story/2019-10-17/south-korea-video-game-addiction-mental-health.

Markey, Patrick M., and Christopher J. Ferguson. *Moral Combat: Why the War on Violent Video Games Is Wrong*. Dallas, TX: BenBella Books, 2017.

"Massively Multiplayer Online Role-Playing Game." *Wikipedia*. Wikimedia Foundation, June 14, 2020. https://en.wikipedia.org/wiki/Massively_multiplayer_online_role-playing_game.

Mayer, Richard E. *Multimedia Learning*. Cambridge University Press, 2001.

Muncy, Julie. "Depression and the Solace of 'Grinding' in Online Games." *Wired*. Conde Nast, July 24, 2019. www.wired.com/story/videogame-grinding-depression/.

Patchin, Justin W. "Are 'Gamers' More Likely to Be 'Bullies'?" *Cyberbullying Research Center*, September 21, 2018. https://cyberbullying.org/are-gamers-more-likely-to-be-bullies.

Publisher. "An Official** Division 46 Statement on the WHO Proposal to Include Gaming Related Disorders in ICD-11." *The Amplifier Magazine*, June 21, 2018. https://div46amplifier.com/2018/06/21/an-official-division-46-statement-on-the-who-proposal-to-include-gaming-related-disorders-in-icd-11/.

"Resolution on Violence in Video Games and Interactive Media." *American Psychological Association*, 2005. www.apa.org/about/policy/interactive-media.pdf.

Robinson, Thomas N., Jorge A. Banda, Lauren Hale, Amy Shirong Lu, Frances Fleming-Milici, Sandra L. Calvert, and Ellen Wartella. "Screen Media Exposure and Obesity in Children and Adolescents." *Pediatrics* 140, no. Supplement 2 (2017). https://doi.org/10.1542/peds.2016-1758k.

Rogers-Whitehead, Carrie. "The Discord with Discord: What Parents Need to Know about the Popular Gamer Chat." *KSL.com*, December 5, 2018. www.ksl.com/article/46441334/the-discord-with-discord-what-parents-need-to-know-about-the-popular-gamer-chat.

Rogers-Whitehead, Carrie. "Loot Boxes: What Parents Need to Know about the Controversial Video Game Craze." *KSL.com*, March 12, 2019. www.ksl.com/article/46509686/loot-boxes-what-parents-need-to-know-about-the-controversial-video-game-craze.

Stanford University. "Virtual Reality Can Help Make People More Empathetic." *Stanford News*, October 16, 2018. https://news.stanford.edu/2018/10/17/virtual-reality-can-help-make-people-empathetic.

Stiller, Anja, Jan Weber, Finja Strube, and Thomas Mößle. "Caregiver Reports of Screen Time Use of Children with Autism Spectrum Disorder: A Qualitative Study." *Behavioral Sciences* 9, no. 5 (2019): 56. https://doi.org/10.3390/bs9050056.

Watson, Amy. "U.S. Media Usage: Time Spent Watching Television 2021." *Statista*, September 11, 2019. www.statista.com/statistics/186833/average-television-use-per-person-in-the-us-since-2002/.

Chapter 8

Resources and Apps
What to Use at Different Developmental Stages

For a caregiver, it can feel overwhelming on how many games, apps, and software are out there. We are inundated with choices, marketing, and opinions on what is best for children. This chapter hopes to help you with decision fatigue and/or confusion about what to choose. There are many good resources out there for children.

Karina Gathu, a parent educator and mother of a young child, said, "I like all the resources and things available to kids. The internet is just a wealth of information, not only for adults, but for kids and teens. There are so many different games and resources. Kids have everything at their fingertips. Yes, that can be scary and potentially bad, but it doesn't have to be."

There are some not-so-good resources out there for children: apps filled with advertisements and hidden microtransactions, software that violates privacy, educational games that offer little to no learning, and video content incorrectly labeled for children. Parents and caregivers can get burned through bad experiences and just prefer not to even try. "We have so many resources," said Gathu. "Weeding them out is a learned skill but we should never not do something because we don't know where to look or how to figure it out" (Rogers-Whitehead, 2020, interview with Karina Gathu). One skill in evaluating media content is critical thinking, looking at the three Cs, and seeing how the content was funded. Another skill is understanding ratings and labels.

Ratings and Labels

Educational Labels

You're looking for a new app for your child's tablet. Browsing through the app store, you read about an app that says it can improve literacy and it's educational. You feel relieved and download the app. But it is truly educational and has it been tested to actually do what it claims it does?

There is no vetting process for an app to label itself "educational." Any developer can do it. "It's easier to get away with calling yourself educational even if there's no way to verify," said Michael Robb, Senior Director of Research with Common Sense Media. "Very, very few companies have the resources to be able to do it. So, a lot of stuff that gets labeled educational is actually aspirational" (Rogers-Whitehead, 2020, interview with Michael Robb).

Well-meaning educators can also use "educational" apps and software in the classroom, not recognizing that they may be helpful. To truly say "This works" from a research standpoint requires time and work. In response to the claim of "educational" found in apps and software, Professor Chris Ferguson, who studies the effects of media, said, "There is no standard definition of what that means. From a researcher's point of view, we want a randomized control, but most companies aren't going to do that. That would be a lot of time and most tech developers don't know how to run a randomized trial."

The time and effort may not be of interest to a developer, who simply wants to make money. By putting a label of educational on the game they can attract more parents and educators who want to help their children learn. In addition, coders, programmers, and developers may know how to code an educational game, but they probably have no background in education or understanding of developmental stages. Some games and shows bring in child psychologists and educators to help create content. For example, PBS employs educators and those who understand child development on their staff. However, that also takes money and time and is not something many content creators can or want to do.

When looking for learning or educational apps and software:

- *Find apps that build skills.* You don't want an app like a worksheet, simply filling in the boxes. Children should have autonomy and choices when using media.
- *Choose apps that give feedback.* It's hard to learn when you don't get feedback on how to improve.
- *Determine who made the app.* Where did the game come from? How is it funded? What other apps did the creator make? Are there any educators and/or child development experts on the

team? Understanding the creators behind the app will help you understand their motivations, and whether they are more interested in making money or teaching children.

Ratings

Ratings can be a guide for parents when determining the best resources for their children. Common Sense Media runs a ratings guide for software, movies, apps, games, and more. What's unique about their ratings is they get a parent rating and a child rating. The ratings between parents and children are often different. For example, in a review for the Amino social networking communities group of apps, an adult reviewer said, "Not safe. . . . We do our best to educate and monitor their internet actions but I learned how easy it is for good kids to be targeted and slowly sucked into participating in a way that is not of their usual character." Contrast that statement with one from a kid who said, "Why Amino is not that bad. To be honest, I feel like all these reviews are over-exaggerating" (Common Sense Media, 2016).

Parents can find other ratings from blogs, industry websites, and word of mouth. The closest thing to "official ratings" for digital media is the Entertainment Software Rating Board (ESRB). They have been assigning ratings to games since 1994 in North America. The ESRB assigns ratings based on game publishers filling out a standardized questionnaire and viewing videos provided by the publisher to trained raters. The ratings should be displayed on game packaging and marketing materials. The ESRB assigns ratings from "E" for everyone to "A" for adults only. They also include content descriptors which "may have triggered a particular rating and/or concern" (ESRB, 2020). Those descriptors include:

- Alcohol reference
- Comic mischief
- Cartoon violence
- Blood and gore
- Drug reference
- Fantasy violence
- Nudity
- Partial nudity
- Language
- Simulated gambling

- Tobacco reference
- Violence

Parents should be aware that the ESRB is a guide, not a law. "The ESRB has no legal consequences for violating it," said Professor Christopher Ferguson. He goes on to say:

> Anything that is government-run comes instantly against the first amendment. Everything we have for government systems is voluntary. Most people think the movie ratings are the government. There is nothing to say that a 3-year-old with a 20-dollar bill can't wander into *The Grudge* and watch that by themselves—there's no law that prevents that to happen. It's the theaters that voluntarily reinforce that. If a police officer sees that 3-year-old in the movie theater there is literally nothing that police officer can do.
>
> (Rogers-Whitehead, 2020, interview with Christopher Ferguson)

The ESRB is not government-run or funded. The board relies on voluntary compliance from tech companies and developers. It also is funded by video game publishers like Activision and EA who pay into the system. These publishers comply with the system because of consumer pressure and marketing.

There has been pressure from some areas for an app rating system similar to the ESRB. But it will run into similar First Amendment concerns. The government can't and won't enforce it. App developers will have to voluntarily opt into the ratings. "There's bazillions of app developers," said Ferguson. "Who would put together a rating system and pay for it? What companies are responsible for paying into the system?" (Rogers-Whitehead, 2020, interview with Christopher Ferguson).

App developers may not have much incentive to pay into that system or turn over their ratings to a third-party organization. Currently, app developers decide the ratings on their own apps. Just as they can decide to label their apps "educational," they can decide the age limits. Why would an app like Snapchat want to rate their app 18 plus when they get more users by having the teen rating?

Globally there is the International Age Rating Coalition (IARC) that works with rating authorities across the world to create rating standards for games and apps. Formed in 2013, it provides a place for developers to have a streamlined classification process. Many countries have their own game rating organizations and the enforcement of those ratings can vary (IARC, 2020).

Parents should review ratings but take them with a grain of salt. What is "harmful" can vary based on the child and the content. Like with the varying reviews on Common Sense Media, someone may see no problem with violence, but have issues with sexual content. Ratings are subjective and based on morals, values, past experience, and more. "Rating systems are only good if they are informing parents. . . . But you don't want to be like 'everything is bad,'" said Ferguson. "I want a gradient" (Rogers-Whitehead, 2020, interview with Christopher Ferguson).

Ratings can lack nuance; they are more black-and-white. People are complicated and changing, and while ratings should inform, they shouldn't make the decision.

Technology for Children Ages 0–8

Ages 0 to 8 are a large span with lots of changes. The suggestions in this section will focus on preschool plus because of recommendations from pediatricians to limit technology below the age of 2. In addition, research on infants and toddlers finds a "transfer deficit," meaning that they learn less from screens and 2D media than they do from in-person instruction until about age 3 (Barr, 2010). For more information and other resources for this age group, see Chapter 3.

Marketing to Children

Marketing has shifted rapidly from the Millennials in their childhood to their children. In previous generations much of the marketing targeted towards children was in television, and farther back, radio. Now the Internet has brought a new platform to advertise to children. Young children in particular are susceptible to these advertisements.

The Federal Trade Commission (FTC) provides regulations on marketing and states, "If you advertise directly to children or market kid-related products to their parents it's important to comply with truth-in-advertising standards." The FTC states, "When consumers see or hear an advertisement, whether it's on the Internet, radio or television, or anywhere else, federal law says that ad must be truthful, not misleading, and when appropriate, backed by scientific evidence" (Advertising and Marketing, 2020).

A 2019 study published in the *Journal of Developmental & Behavioral Pediatrics* found through a pilot program of children ages 1–5 found that of the 135 apps reviewed, 95% contained at least one type of advertising (Meyer et al., 2019). The different categories of advertising include (ranked most to least prevalent):

1. Commercial characters
2. Full-app teasers
3. Advertising videos interrupting play
4. Prompts to rate the app
5. Distracting ads like banners
6. Hidden ads camouflaged in game play

These advertisements were "significantly more prevalent in free apps (100% vs 88% of paid apps) but occurred at similar rates in apps labeled as 'educational' versus other categories" (Meyer et al., 2019).

Online influencers are another way through which children are marketed to. In Fall of 2019 watchdog group Truth in Advertising filed a complained with the FTC about the formal YouTube channel Ryan ToysReview (Truth in Advertising, 2020). In these videos Ryan, a 7-year-old, opens new toys and tries them out. By the time of the lawsuit these videos had over thirty billion views. According to a *New York Times* article about the lawsuit, there is sponsored content that is not clearly labeled as an advertisement. "A 5-year-old isn't going to understand that Ryan's talking about the toys because Target is paying him to talk about the toys. There may be some disclosure, but disclosure isn't meaningful to a child that young," said Josh Golin with the nonprofit Commercial-Free Childhood in the article (Hsu, 2019).

These influencers can be found on many other channels online targeted to children. TikTok stars, Twitch streamers, and more may be sponsored by companies unbeknownst to the viewer. Commercial-Free Childhood argues against this marketing and play that is "driven by branded toys, media and storylines." They say that "children's values are shaped by marketing messages" instead of their families and communities (Commercial Free Childhood, 2020). Parents may spend time reviewing and evaluating apps for young children, but not consider the advertisements that may appear in those apps. There is no independent review board for child-targeted ads. Parents can help avoid these ads by purchasing apps instead of using free versions. More importantly, parents and caregivers should have discussions with children at a young age about what an advertisement is, and what it's trying to do.

Platforms and Tech for Young Children

Joi Podgorny is the founder of Good People Solutions, a consulting firm that helps companies leverage technology to help with their culture. She also worked in tech and creating platforms for parents and children. When asked what the trends for younger children are, she said, "We might see more kid-specific communities. What I've seen in the last five years is making all ages communities, like a *Fortnite*." Children, even young children, want to be more like their older peers; they look up to them and don't always like to be relegated to the "kid's table." While there have been some kid-specific platforms in the past, notably Club Penguin, which was most active between 2007–2013, around the mid 2010s there were less kid-specific social platforms and more spaces in teen and adult games for children. Podgorny said about the publishers of content, "Kids are playing teen and adult games; they're having to make accommodations to their offerings . . . because the kids are there they're spending money and active participants. The producers of those brands could easily say no kids allowed, which is what they used to do, but now they're making accommodations" (Rogers-Whitehead, 2020, interview with Joi Podgorny).

With the COVID-19 lockdown and more children at families at home, things may shift for more communities for younger children. "There was a hands-off period in the last 5 years like, 'well *Fortnite* seems fine,'" said Podgorny. But kids want to be with the older crowd. "I've seen a lot of 9- and 10-year-olds playing *Fortnite* and they get bored with that game plan and want to play *Overwatch* and *Call of Duty*. . . . I anticipate at least some attempt at some kid-centric communities in future years" (Rogers-Whitehead, 2020, interview with Joi Podgorny).

What this means for parents is that younger children are in spaces with older children. While of course there were older kids and even the rare adult in kid-specific communities like Club Penguin, the interface and chat were extremely locked down. When children are in spaces for all ages, it means parents need to utilize settings, monitor more, and have those conversations about not sharing personal information.

Merve Lapus, VP of Outreach and National Partnerships with Common Sense Media and father of two, says not to worry too much about these platforms. "The research shows that most kids even though they see that these things are happening, they're not engaged in it. Platforms have been built to share this type of contact . . . you set a level of protection and safety so that you can use these platforms for these great opportunities" (Rogers-Whitehead, 2020, interview with Merve Lapus).

Some suggestions for monitoring and protecting children on these platforms include:

- Limiting or blocking any direct messages or chat requests from non-friends/contacts.
- Setting subscriptions to private. On some platforms private subscriptions or privacy settings are only available for paid accounts. If this is the case, consider making a paid account.
- Create private servers/rooms for children. For example, on *Minecraft* users can create a private server and give the server's IP address to friends and family and people they can trust.
- Filter language. Some games and software, like *Fortnite*, have parental controls that will filter adult language. For voice chat however, this is not an option.

What are some platforms and options for young children for media? Podgorny suggests parents look at larger companies/networks:

"I think the big networks are always the best places to go because they have been and will always be targeting that demographic." (Rogers-Whitehead, 2020, interview with Joi Podgorny)

Unfortunately, there is a lack of research on newer technologies and young children. With that lack of data, parents may want to utilize the tried and tested media channels and outlets.

Some recommendations of technology and media for young children include:

- *PBS.* The Public Broadcasting Service is a US nonprofit and the most well-known and prominent provider of educational television programming. In recent years PBS has provided more online content directed at young children. Their PBS Kids products aimed at ages 0–12 are more vetted educational apps and do not have ads. They also have filtered and kid-specific videos online that are an alternative to YouTube Kids. Every state has a local affiliate with over 300 television stations operated by other nonprofits, state agencies, universities, or other local organizations.

- *Nick Jr.* Nickelodeon (Nick) is a private US media corporation, the first cable TV channel for children launched in 1979. Nick Jr is their programming aimed at ages 2–5. Nick Jr has an app with video content, learning, and preschool games. Nick Jr also offers Noggin, a subscription with ad-free shows and content designed by educational experts. However, these games and shows have character and marketing content, like its popular show *Paw Patrol*. Nick Jr doesn't just want children to watch the shows, but buy the shirts, toys, shoes, and more.

- *Disney Junior.* Like Nickelodeon, Disney is a private corporation and it also offers programming for young children in Disney Junior. Disney Junior launched in 2010 and is aimed at preschoolers. DisneyNOW is a universal Disney app which includes Disney Junior. The Disney Junior app includes video content and games based on Disney characters. Disney, like other private companies making content for young children, want to create brand loyalty (Disney-Now, 2020).

- *Government-funded resources.* Government-funded sources of media are more likely to have fewer advertisements and less bias. They are not motivated by money as much as private enterprises. One example is the British Broadcasting Corporation (BBC). The BBC runs Bitesize, which is educational content for kids. Bitesize offers daily lessons, programs, and more. The BBC also runs MUZZY, which teaches kids other languages and has existed for over thirty years. NPR, or National Public Radio, also offers content and media for kids. Radiolab for Kids is a repository of family-friendly content; and NPR also runs *Wow in the World*, a podcast for ages 5–12 that talks about science and technology.

Technology for Children Ages 8–13

The tween years, between childhood and adolescence, are fraught with change and transition, but also a fun time of bonding. Puberty begins at these ages, which changes bodies and minds. Tweens are much more focused on their peers and how they look to others, and are pulling away from parents and caregivers. They are highly influenced by trends, the desire to fit in and look a certain way, and technology can magnify these influences and the influencers. This section will talk about some of those influences as well as the growth of homework and responsibilities, and provide a list of suggestions. For further suggestions and information on the tween years, see Chapter 4.

Homework

For children in the early grades of elementary school, there may be no homework at all. Then around third, fourth, or fifth grade in most schools children find themselves taking home packets and logging on for assignments. According to a survey of over a thousand teachers through the University of Phoenix, both high school and middle school teachers assigned roughly the same amount of homework each week: three and a half hours. If a student in middle or high school has five classes, that's three and a half hours of homework each *day*. There is a jump in homework assignments during the tween years. Elementary teachers assign about three hours of homework each week, but since younger students typically have just one teacher, there is far less per day (Stainburn, 2014).

At these ages, homework can be stressful for both parents and children. Younger children are developing self-regulation skills; they are new to homework and don't always understand time management. In addition, many of these children are asked to log in and do digital assignments, without having the digital literacy skills or any of that instruction. I've seen this in my own home this past year. My 8-year-old has been given assignments on an online learning platform to develop reading and writing skills. However, to be able to access and utilize the content online, he has to have a baseline of reading and writing skills. Logging in, troubleshooting, finding assignments, answering assignments—all of them require the very skills the platform is tasked to develop. Thus, much of the homework falls on me, who knows how to navigate the interface and fully read and understand the assignments.

The use of digital materials in classrooms continues to rise (Pusey, 2019). According to market research with the firm Simba, about 60% of instructional materials in schools are digital as of 2019. Many courses use a mix of textbooks, online content, subscriptions, and other supplemental materials. According to an analyst at Simba, most literacy materials are in print form, while math and science are more likely to be digital (Simba Information, 2020). There are advantages to digital materials. They can be updated more quickly and teachers can more easily grade and track progress on assignments. However, there are concerns about the quality of the learning, access, digital citizenship concerns, and more.

Merve Lapus, in addition to his work with Common Sense Media, has two school-aged girls at home. In his home, homework can be a stressor. To help establish a routine and get the homework done, Lapus said, "The reality is that homework needs to be done before you go out and play." He recommends "setting a structure for after school . . . you're more effective if you're in that frame of mine." Families may also be concerned about screen time, discussed more in Chapter 6. Lapus said not to conflate all screen time together. "With the digital side of things there's a lot of concerns from families to find this media balance. But everything they need to do is online. . . . Not all screen time is created equal" (Rogers-Whitehead, 2020, interview with Merve Lapus).

Other suggestions for making homework with tweens less stressful include:

- *Using timers.* Get a visual clock or use some other kind of timer to denote a start and end of homework. Aim for short bursts of intense focus rather than long periods of work. Focus is a muscle that children need to develop.
- *Having a designated homework space.* Part of focus and work is getting in the right mindset. It's harder to focus if we are on the couch where we watch TV, or in the bed where we sleep. Have a specific area of the home just for homework and learning and try not to let other tasks occur in that space.
- *Providing snacks.* Kids can be hungry after school. Put out snacks in their homework space so hunger doesn't distract them from work.
- *Creating a list of passwords and logins.* Passwords for accounts will be forgotten. Make a physical list and save a digital copy of all the logins and passwords for homework accounts.

- *Providing ambient noise.* Put on instrumentals or other ambient noise in the background. Do not use a TV since that can be more distracting.
- *Limiting tabs.* Limit the number of tabs that can be on your child's computer. There are browser plugins that will do this for you. Have them focus on one assignment and task at a time.
- *Tracking usage.* If you are concerned that your child is losing focus and using other apps instead of doing homework, there are apps and software that can track the usage. If your child is using a learning management system (LMS), there are dashboards that will track the minutes on assignments.

These homework issues are also one of circumstance. Many children do not have the devices or broadband access to successfully complete their homework. According to Pew Research, approximately 15% of households with school-age children do not have the Internet at home. These students may have to finish a paper on a mobile phone or go to a library in the evening to print out a document (Auxier, 2020). These students may have parents at home that do not speak English or have the digital literacy skills to assist them when there are technology issues. Their parents also may be working and unavailable to answer homework questions. This equity gap between students is called the homework gap, and it has been exacerbated by the COVID-19 shutdown in Spring of 2020.

According to *EdWeek*, forty-eight states, four US territories, and other private and charter schools have shut down for the 2019–2020 year as of May 2020 (Education Week, 2020). These closures have affected the whole world affecting millions of school-aged children. Schools have moved to online learning, which leaves out many students. Angela Siefer, executive director of the National Digital Inclusion Alliance, said in a *Citylab* article, "The inequities in all of our education systems are going to be even worse. The kids whose families do not have internet connection are going to have at least some learning continuing during this period, and the kids who don't won't" (Poon, 2020).

For families who do not have Internet access, there are some resources for online homework:

- *Libraries and recreation centers.* Many libraries offer 24/7 WiFi that can be accessed in the parking lot after closures. They can also provide homework help in addition to scanners, copy machines, and other devices.

- *Comcast Essentials.* Comcast offers high speed Internet at no or low cost to households who qualify along with subsidized devices.
- *AT&T Broadband Now.* Like Comcast, AT&T provides a low-cost broadband access option to households that qualify.
- *Lifeline Support.* This is a US federal program that connects individuals that qualify with the lowest-price Internet.

Online Privacy

The growth of online homework can impact children's privacy. COPPA, the Children's Online Privacy Protection Act, is a US federal law that mandates that commercial online services provide notice of consent before any personal data is collected. COPPA also must allow parents to opt out of further data collection and maintain the confidentiality of any children's information that's collected (Herold, 2018). Some states and school districts may have additional children's privacy laws. In addition, there are standards with GDPR, the General Data Protection Regulation, in the European Union.

For parents, there is less control over their children's privacy when it comes to homework. The FTC says that in some situations "schools may act as the parent's agent and can consent to the collection of kids' information on the parent's behalf" (Herold, 2018). Schools are often responsible for making sure all the privacy laws are followed and getting that consent, not the technology vendors. In addition, many online learning materials have third-party trackers or other software embedded into their services that may not be disclosed to schools. Even if a school turns down a platform or an app, that doesn't always mean a teacher won't use it in their classroom. A parent might not know that these apps or services are not approved by the school or district and that they may collect personal information from their children.

Schools should send parents an acceptable-use policy or other similar document at the beginning of the school year. This should describe what information would be collected and used. This is an opportunity for parents to inquire and express their concerns. Parents and caregivers should also have conversations with their children about how websites and other software can track usage and collect data, and caution children to not share private information publicly.

Platforms and Tech for Tweens

Young people during the tween years are transitioning from children to teenager, from one teacher in school to six, from caring what their parents think to caring what their friends think. There are many emotions during these transitions and technology can magnify them. Parents should manage the devices and watch closely how media is affecting their tween. There are some games and apps that can cause more confusion and some that give connection.

Merve Lapus sees these strong feelings in his own children who like to be on their iPads. "Overcoming the challenges of transitioning on and off shouldn't be as hard if you recognize what we're transitioning from. If you're transitioning from something fun and bright and colorful and fast paced to something you know is going to be hard." Homework battles exist in part because children may love to play games or chat with friends in bright and shiny platforms with lots of response and movement, then their parents ask them to sit and do homework which may consist of reading long passages, clicking through text, or other activities that may seem dull in comparison. Lapus suggests saying, "Okay, now we've done this and now it's time for you to be creative and figure it out." He encourages parents to let their older children have downtime. "Being bored is an important problem-solving time" (Rogers-Whitehead, 2020, interview with Merve Lapus).

Textbox 8.1

Among younger children and tweens, *Roblox* is a popular multiplayer online game that has grown since it came out in 2006. *Roblox* is similar to *LEGO* and *Minecraft* in that it is a game creation platform that utilizes LEGO-like blocks. Players have different options in *Roblox*: to play games designed by others or create their own. *Roblox* has its own game-developing tool that can even gain money for creators by charging others to play. Most younger kids just want to play, and they have many, many games to choose from. These games can range from puzzles, to first-person shooters, to adventure, and anything else you can think of.

Some of the pros of *Roblox* include:

- *Educational tool:* The game creation software is a fun learning tool for kids.
- *Entertaining: Roblox* offers a wide variety of games for all ages of kids.
- *Parental settings: Roblox* offers parental settings for their chat functions and those with whom their kids can interact.

There are potential cons of *Roblox*, which include:

- *Costs: Roblox* has in-game purchases and a currency called Robux that's required for certain games and settings. While Robux is free, kids will be inundated with ads to buy Robux.
- *Chat functions:* There is a Chat & Party function with *Roblox*, and although chatting for kids under 13 is filtered, issues of language and content can arise.
- *Time: Roblox* is a game that does not end. There are always things to do. Kids may play too much *Roblox* at the expense of other activities.

Build in that quiet time and spaces where there are no screens. When it is time for screens, consider these suggestions:

- *Mindfulness and calming apps.* These apps can assist with transitions for tweens, bedtime routines, and more. Some popular ones are Calm, Buddhify, or HappiMe aimed at young people. For more information about these types of apps, see Chapter 6.
- *Educational apps to support learning.* Children these ages are starting to get their own phones. Part of the discussions into getting a phone can be about educational apps. Some educational apps/games to consider are DuoLingo (free language lessons), Civilization (history), The Infinite Arcade (game design), and Spelling City.
- *Disney XD.* This sister division of the Disney Channel is focused on ages 6 to 14. It replaced Toon Disney in 2009. It has a great

deal of action adventure titles and anime. Like Disney Junior, Disney XD offers games, videos, and more through its app. Disney XD has branded characters and advertising content that can encourage children to ask their parents to spend money.

- *Nickelodeon.* Nickelodeon (Nick) is the private parent company that includes Nick Jr. While Nick Jr is focused on preschool-aged children, most of the content of Nickelodeon is aimed at older children and young teenagers. The content includes made-for-TV movies, cartoons, mobile apps, a radio station, and magazine.

Technology for Teens Ages 13–18

The teenage years are busy ones. Adolescents are working in school, often working in jobs, and doing the labor of developing their real-life and digital identities. In addition, teens are reaching sexual maturity and have more interest in romantic and sexual relationships, and their bodies are preparing them for leaving the home. Parents have less control over the media their teens watch, but still have an important role. As well as being a trusting adult and source of wisdom, parents can also encourage technology and media that prepares them for the future. In a few short years their children, now adults, will be out of the house. Those young adults will be judged and evaluated not just by their real-life identities but who they are online.

YouTube and Becoming a Creator

As children age, the mindset of parents needs to shift from regulating content to encouraging young people to create their own content. The ability to go beyond knowledge to application is an important 21st-century skill. In a 2019 Brookings Institution article the authors write,

> Education in the 21st century is not the same as education in the 20th century . . . in both centuries, education has been the main mechanism for individuals to gain core knowledge and concepts. However, now society demands that education systems equip students with the ability to go beyond learning core knowledge and concepts to using and applying them.
>
> (Helyn et al., 2019)

A family is one education system. Although homes do not typically have formalized education, they're a place where students can create, explore, and apply knowledge.

Technology provides opportunities to create, but more often we consume. An example of this is YouTube, the second-most-visited site in the world and a popular platform for Gen Z and Generation Alpha. A 2019 *Washington Post* report stated that "more than twice as many young people watch videos every day as did four years ago, and the average time spent watching videos—mostly on YouTube— has roughly doubled, to an hour each day" (Siegel, 2019). Those stats were from a Common Sense Media report. Another finding was the lack of time in creation. Teens and other young people simply watch YouTube; they're not interacting with it. Chatting, reading online, and creating content like music or art was just 2% of the time spent with videos.

In the knowledge economy, workers cannot simply consume information, they need to evaluate, disseminate, and create it. Watching a video on woodworking may give you some more knowledge, but it doesn't mean you know how to make something with wood. There are many DIY and educational videos on YouTube. YouTube has created a learning channel for teens and adults called "Learning" (YouTube, 2020). There are also easy-to-use video editing tools on YouTube and making a creator account is free. The opportunities are there, but the pull of entertaining and fast-moving content is strong. At these ages parents should encourage this shift of watching to exploring, scrolling to explaining, and consuming to creating.

Textbox 8.2

LinkedIn is a social network for working professionals and is one of the most popular social platforms with over 675 million monthly users in 2020 (Omnicore, 2020). LinkedIn also allows members as young as 13. Some benefits for teenagers being part of LinkedIn include:

- *College selection.* LinkedIn's University Pages are a great source of information about colleges. These pages can tell you who the school's alumni are, what careers they had after attending this particular college, and more.

- *Motivation.* On LinkedIn you can follow hashtags of careers, individuals, companies, and more. If a young person has a particular interest in a career field, they can follow the professionals in that field and get valuable insights. People can also follow motivational hashtags and thought leaders to help them focus and reach their goals.
- *Job searching.* Many companies use LinkedIn to recruit interns and job candidates. There are also positions posted on LinkedIn that may not be found other places. A teen may find their first job or internship through LinkedIn.
- *Space to stand out.* LinkedIn is like an interactive job portfolio. It's a permanent resume that can evolve over time. By creating a presence on LinkedIn, teens can get into the mindset of developing a professional digital identity and practice of managing their career.

In addition to the career and college benefits, parents and caregivers can feel assured that it is far less likely that their teen will be harassed online or exposed to uncomfortable content on LinkedIn. It's a space for professionals, resumes, and people who are trying to look their best.

Platforms and Tech for Teens

During the COVID-19 stay-at-home orders, TikTok, the social video creation/sharing platform grew exponentially. TikTok is aimed at tweens and teens and can be a bewildering place for adults. Joi Podgorny said, "One thing I love is that teens are teaching their parents on TikTok these dances. . . . It's a fun thing and it's a way to engage with kids" (Rogers-Whitehead, 2020, interview with Joi Podgorny).

Teens are teaching parents how to make their own videos and joining them in dance moves or other content. Parents, particularly mothers, having newfound TikTok skills, are sharing their own content using hashtags like #momsoftiktok or #over30. Adolescents have a lot to share with adults, if adults will listen. These are some recommendations of tech for teens to help them prepare for the future. However, be sure to ask *their* recommendations as well.

- *Financial literacy.* There are some teen-focused apps and software out there to help adolescents save money for college or other goals. YNAB (You Need a Budget) is a Gen Z-focused and simple-to-use budget software available across different apps and platforms. The app Mint also helps with budgets, savings, payments, and more. Toshl is a finance tracking app that can analyze spending habits and has a teen-friendly interface.

- *Sexual education.* Planned Parenthood has a sex-ed chatbot named Roo that allows anyone to ask questions for free. Planned Parenthood also has a "For Teens" website with games, resources, and more.
- *Time management.* Teens are balancing more responsibilities, and in college they'll need to handle even more on their own. Consider getting a time management/organizational app like Evernote, Google Keep, Wunderlist, Notebook, or Trello.
- *Educational apps to support learning.* Encourage teen creativity with apps like GarageBand, Popplet, TED, Lumosity, WattPad, and Animoto. There are many different ones out there, so let your teen's interests guide your suggestions.
- *Mood tracking.* Emotions can go up and down during the teen years. Mood tracking apps can help teens self-reflect and examine their feelings. By tracking when and why the feelings occur, adolescents can better self-regulate. Some suggestions of mood tracker apps include Daylio, Worry Watch, RealifeChange, and MindShift.

Resources for Parents

This chapter has shared resources and recommendations for children and teens, but what about parents? Where do parents go when they want to find out about technology, apps, games, and more?

Merve Lapus, a VP with Common Sense Media, shares his experience with the nonprofit concerning resources: "We first started using the term digital citizenship 10–11 years ago, but the idea around media balance, mental health opened up a space. And when you open up that space you see lots of people flood in" (Rogers-Whitehead, 2020, interview with Merve Lapus).

The area of digital parenting and digital citizenship is new and multidisciplinary. You have people from different fields and perspectives offering recommendations and resources that may not always align with your family's values. These resources may simply be one of opinion, without any research or data behind them.

Lapus recommends parents and caregivers to follow the money: "As a parent you want to figure out where they're coming from.

Where's the tone and tenor of the organization?" He gives the example of curriculum about life skills developed by Philip Morris, the tobacco company (Rogers-Whitehead, 2020, interview with Merve Lapus).

Both Philip Morris and another tobacco company, Brown and Williamson, started working in 1999 to promote a Life Skills Training (LST) program, "a school-based drug prevention program recommended by the Centers for Disease Control and Prevention to reduce youth smoking." Through their work to disseminate that program into schools, the tobacco companies "hired a public relations firm to promote LST and a separate firm to evaluate the program. The evaluation conducted for the two companies did not show that LST was effective at reducing smoking after the first or second year of implementing the program. Even so, the tobacco companies continued to award grants to schools for the program" (Mandel et al., 2006). Educators and parents may assume that a free program called "life skills training" has good intent, but if they knew the funding source, they may be more wary.

Organizations that recommend apps or resources may be funded by those resources. I know from my personal experience running Digital Respons-Ability that we have been contacted over email and Instagram by companies asking us to test out and share about our product to families we work with. I never recommend specific products in my trainings, although when asked or when I write, I may share my opinions. A regular request we get through email is to link to other companies. These links, called affiliate links, are URLs that are meant to pass traffic on to affiliate products. Companies that use affiliate links can increase their visibility in search engines and some may receive a commission if someone clicks on that link and it leads to a sale. If you are looking for recommendations of resources and find a blog crammed with URLs, be suspicious that this blogger may have different motivations for recommending certain products.

When evaluating reviews and parent resources, ask the same questions you would want your child to ask. "You need to do the work yourself to dive deeper as we are urging our kids to dig deeper into vetting resources. You're not just diving deep into the content, you're doing lateral reading and lateral research," said Lapus (Rogers-Whitehead, 2020, interview with Merve Lapus).

Lateral reading is reading multiple sources side by side, instead of examining one source for veracity. Some questions to ask when conducting lateral research include:

- When was this created?
- How is this funded? Is it transparent who funds the resource?
- Who is the author? Is it a bot or an actual person?
- To whom do the authors refer and link?
- How many advertisements are on the site? And are the advertisements transparent?
- What does this organization want you to do?

Joi Podgorny recommends parents find other parents when they have questions about technology. "I would recommend finding parent communities as opposed to finding a one-stop shop. . . . Go one step further, sure reference Common Sense Media but try to find a community of parents that you can kind of vent to and share experiences with. There's always going to be one of those in the groups that have done all the research that's going to be more helpful to you psychologically and logistically as the landscape evolves as it does." Technology moves quickly; games have continual updates; apps come and go and trends with tweens and teens change rapidly. This means that parents may need more updated recommendations. "You have to seek out people and know that the landscape evolves," said Podgorny. "If you read an article about *Fortnite* three years ago, you're not going to be there. *Fortnite*'s doing different stuff right now. Your kid is doing the stuff that *Fortnite* is doing right now" (Rogers-Whitehead, 2020, interview with Joi Podgorny).

Another suggestion to find resources is follow hashtags. These hashtags should appear on multiple platforms and can pull together up-to-date information on media. If a hashtag is trending and used more, that's a sign that it's popular—or controversial. Find hashtags that align with your values and interests. There are sites like *best-hashtags.com* that rank popular and new hashtags and show the most used hashtags around topics.

Parents can also get involved in communities through popular platforms. "Facebook has their own digital citizenship place. *Roblox* has their place coming from civility," said Lapus. But he cautioned that "you should know that they are coming from a perspective that you want your time on the platform" (Rogers-Whitehead, 2020, interview with Merve Lapus).

However, parents can get guides to how games work, how to set controls, and other advice on the various "parent guides" and communities on major social media platforms and games.

The authors of *Moral Combat: Why the War on Violent Video Games is Wrong* write, "A source of purely objective information simply doesn't exist. Information is filtered by politics, money, moral crusades, personal egos, and hosts of tangled biases and assumptions. What comes out on the other end of the process is rarely objective, verifiable fact" (Markey and Ferguson, 2017). Ratings, reviews, and media content have both pros and cons. Reviewers have their own biases, perspectives, and motivations for what they say. Ratings organizations also have reasons why they rate as they do. An app that comes highly recommended from a parent may receive mixed reviews from their kid. This chapter just shared a small fraction of what's available and others may see these recommendations differently. There is no perfect piece of technology, app, or media. They all have their flaws and can affect individuals differently. Parents can spend hours scouring reviews and talking to other parents, but the best way to evaluate content for your child is to know your child.

Summary Points: Resources and Apps

- There is no regulation on "educational apps" and parents should be aware that just because it is labeled educational does not mean it's vetted to do what it claims.
- Ratings organizations like the ESRB are not the law, but a guide.
- There are regulations on marketing to children that in the US are regulated by the Federal Trade Commission. However, online with influencers and other content it can be difficult to determine what is marketing and what is not.
- Good media for young children includes government-funded media organizations like the BBC or PBS. Limit media for children 2 and younger.
- For tweens, online homework can be a stressful issue. Over 60% of instructional materials are online. There is a great increase in the hours of homework from elementary to middle school.
- There are online privacy laws, like COPPA, that prevent companies from taking data from children under 13.

- Good media for tweens includes educational software and mindfulness apps.
- Parents should encourage teens to create content for future employers and to increase chances of college admission.
- Good media for teens includes apps and software for financial literacy, sexual education, time management, and mood tracking.
- When determining appropriate resources for children, parents should examine the funding sources of media. They should also engage in lateral reading, evaluating reviews from multiple sources. Finally, parents should follow certain hashtags and consider joining parent communities online to find the best resources.

References

"About the International Age Rating Coalition: IARC." About the International Age Rating Coalition | IARC. www.globalratings.com/about.aspx (Accessed May 5, 2020).

"Advertising and Marketing | Federal Trade Commission." *Federal Trade Commission.* www.ftc.gov/tips-advice/business-center/advertising-and-marketing (Accessed May 5, 2020).

Auxier, Brooke, and Monica Anderson. "As Schools Close Due to the Coronavirus, Some U.S. Students Face a Digital 'Homework Gap'." *Pew Research Center*, March 16, 2020. www.pewresearch.org/fact-tank/2020/03/16/as-schools-close-due-to-the-coronavirus-some-u-s-students-face-a-digital-homework-gap/.

Barr, R. "Transfer of Learning between 2D and 3D Sources during Infancy: Informing Theory and Practice." *Developmental Review: DR* 30, no. 2 (2010): 128–154. https://doi.org/10.1016/j.dr.2010.03.001.

"Digital Media Projected to Capture 60.1% Share of PreK-12 Instructional Materials in 2019." *Simba Information.* www.simbainformation.com/Content/Blog/2019/08/08/Digital-Media-Projected-to-Capture-601-Share-of-PreK-12-Instructional-Materials-in-2019 (Accessed May 11, 2020).

"DisneyNow." *Disneynow.go.com.* https://disneynow.com/apps (Accessed May 5, 2020).

Ferguson, Christopher. Conversation with the author March 2020.

Gathu, Karina. Conversation with the author April 2020.

Helyn, Kim, Esther Care, and Alvin Vista. "Education Systems Need Alignment for Teaching and Learning 21st Century Skills." *Brookings*, January 30, 2019. www.brookings.edu/blog/education-plus-development/

2019/01/30/education-systems-need-alignment-for-teaching-and-learning-21st-century-skills/.

Herold, Benjamin. "COPPA and Schools: The (Other) Federal Student Privacy Law, Explained." *Education Week*, October 12, 2018. www.edweek.org/ew/issues/childrens-online-privacy-protection-act-coppa/index.html.

"Home." *Campaign for Commercial Free Childhood*, May 27, 2020. https://commercialfreechildhood.org/.

"Home." *ESRB Ratings*. www.esrb.org/ (Accessed April 28, 2020).

Hsu, Tiffany. "Popular YouTube Toy Review Channel Accused of Blurring Lines for Ads." *The New York Times*, September 4, 2019. www.nytimes.com/2019/09/04/business/media/ryan-toysreview-youtube-ad-income.html.

Kievlan, Patricia Monticello. "Kid Reviews for Amino-Communities, Chat, Forums, and Groups: Common Sense Media." *Common Sense Media*. Common Sense Media: Ratings, Reviews, and Advice, August 1, 2016. www.commonsensemedia.org/app-reviews/amino-communities-chat-forums-and-groups/user-reviews/child.

Lapus, Merve. Conversation with the author April 2020.

"Learning." *YouTube*. www.youtube.com/channel/UCtFRv9O2AHqOZjjynzrv-xg/about (Accessed May 5, 2020).

"LinkedIn by the Numbers: Stats Demographics and Fun Facts." Omnicore, February 10, 2020. www.omnicoreagency.com/linkedin-statistics/.

Mandel, Lev L., Stella Aguinaga Bialous, and Stanton A. Glantz. "Avoiding 'Truth': Tobacco Industry Promotion of Life Skills Training." *Journal of Adolescent Health* 39, no. 6 (2006): 868–879. https://doi.org/10.1016/j.jadohealth.2006.06.010.

"Map: Coronavirus and School Closures." *Education Week*, March 6, 2020. www.edweek.org/ew/section/multimedia/map-coronavirus-and-school-closures.html.

Markey, Patrick M., and Christopher J. Ferguson. *Moral Combat: Why the War on Violent Video Games Is Wrong*. Dallas, TX: BenBella Books, 2017.

Meyer, Marisa, Victoria Adkins, Nalingna Yuan, Heidi M. Weeks, Yung-Ju Chang, and Jenny Radesky. "Advertising in Young Children's Apps." *Journal of Developmental & Behavioral Pediatrics* 40, no. 1 (2019): 32–39. https://doi.org/10.1097/dbp.0000000000000622.

Podgorny, Joi. Conversation with the author May 2020.

Poon, Linda. "Coronavirus Exposes How Bad America's Homework Gap Really Is." *CityLab*, March 22, 2020. www.citylab.com/equity/2020/03/coronavirus-online-schools-homework-internet-access-homework/608116/.

Pusey, Stacey. "Digital Instructional Materials, OER Rising in PreK-12 Classrooms." *EdScoop*, October 4, 2019. https://edscoop.com/digital-instructional-materials-oer-rising-in-prek-12-classrooms/.

Robb, Michael. Conversation with the author March 2020.

Siegel, Rachel. "Tweens, Teens and Screens: The Average Time Kids Spend Watching Online Videos Has Doubled in 4 Years." *The Washington Post*. WP Company, October 29, 2019. www.washingtonpost.com/technology/2019/10/29/survey-average-time-young-people-spend-watching-videos-mostly-youtube-has-doubled-since/.

Stainburn, Samantha. "High Schools Assign 3.5 Hours of Homework a Night, Survey Estimates." *Education Week: Time and Learning*, February 28, 2014. http://blogs.edweek.org/edweek/time_and_learning/2014/02/high_schools_assign_3.5_hours.html.

"Truth in Advertising." *Federal Trade Commission*, May 7, 2020. www.ftc.gov/news-events/media-resources/truth-advertising.

Appendix

Conversation Starters and Questions to Ask a Child About Technology

Ages 0–8

- Show me how do you do that on (name of the device).
- What is your favorite thing to do on (name of the device)?
- What do you think will happen next in the (movie/show/game)?
- When I'm on my phone how does it make you feel?
- May I have your permission to share this (picture/video/quote) of yours?
- How did it make you feel when you saw that on (movie/show/game)?

Ages 8–13

- What things are private to you? What things are public?
- Will you be able to finish your homework on time to (play game/watch show)?
- Who are your friends online?
- Do those friends ever do things that make you uncomfortable? What do you do when you feel uncomfortable?
- What are some things you like to do online with me and the rest of your family? What is something we do that you don't like?
- How do you feel about how much time I spend online? How can I improve?
- How would you feel if someone shared something private about you online without your permission? Have I ever done that?

Ages 13–18

- What do you think that (show/movie/meme/etc.) is trying to say? Why do you think it's saying that?

- What would you tell a friend who shared something online that probably should have been kept private?
- If a friend told you that you shared something that should have been private, or made them feel uncomfortable, how would you feel?
- How does technology affect dating relationships? What do you see?
- What's something positive you can do online today?
- Who do you want to be online?

The following pages are family media plan flowcharts developed by the author with guidance from the American Academy of Pediatrics. They can help families create their own norms around common technology issues at home.

Model

A Family Media Plan Guide For 0-6 Year Old Children

DIGITAL RESPONS-ABILITY
EDUCATE-INFORM-EMPOWER

Screen Time

Does your child own their own device?

YES → **How much time do they spend on their devices?**

The American Academy of Pediatrics recommends no screen time under 18 months and limited video chats and interactive touch screens from 18 months to 2 years old. There are not specific screen time recommendations for other ages

NO → **Are screens interfering with family or other social time?**

NO →

Is the device interfering with social or language development?

YES → The first three years of life is the most intensive period of developing speech and language skills according to the National Institutes of Health. Screens can get in the way of this development and should be very limited the first three years of life

NO → Devices are wonderful ways to connect young children with far away friends and relatives. They can also be a tool for learning although make sure to read the reviews and recommendations because app ratings are determined by the developer, not an unbiased educator. Media can also be a way for parent and child to bond. Point out things you see on screens; ask your child questions. At these ages screens should be limited and interactive.

Do they share a device with a friend of family member?

YES → Sharing a device can keep young children safe since you can see what they're doing. However, it can also mean that children are accidentally exposed to inappropriate content. If you share a device with your child make sure your history/cache is cleared and that you have parental settings on content they can access.

NO

Screen-Free Areas & Times

What areas of your home are screens not allowed? Select below:

☐ Kitchen table
☐ Living room
☐ Bedrooms

What time of the day do screens and mobile devices get turned off? Select below:

☐ Two hours before bed
☐ One hour before bed
☐ Right before bed

Social and emotional development is crucial at these ages. Your child models your behavior. They need opportunities to interact with you. Try to keep screens away from areas of family conversation, particularly the kitchen table.

Screens can interfere with sleep. The American Academy of Pediatrics recommends:
Infants 4 months to 1 year: 12-16 hours a day
Children 1-2 years should sleep 11 to 14 hours a day
Children 3-5 years should sleep 10-13 hours a day
Children 6-12 years should sleep 9-12 hours a day
They also recommend screens be turned off at least half an hour before bed.

YES ← Do you have screen free times at meals? → NO

Media Consumption

When you and your child have recreational screen time you (check any of the below):

☐ Watch media with your child
☐ Play together with apps or video games
☐ Video chat with friends or relatives

If none, what is one that you are or could be doing now?

Children learn better from media when they share the experience with an adult. Watching and playing together can help you stay connected with your child, and helps keep them safe.

Digital citizenship

Digital citizenship is the ethical and responsible use of technology. Here are some digital citizenship rules for teens: (check any of the rules you follow in your own home)

☐ Limit screen time
☐ Ask a parent or caregiver permission to use their device
☐ Ask a parent or caregiver to chat or play an online game
☐ Turn off devices at least 30 minutes before bed

References: American Academy of Pediatrics (Copyright © 2016) - Council on Communications and Media Digital Citizenship. Teaching Strategies and Practice from the Field by Carrie Rogers-Whitehead

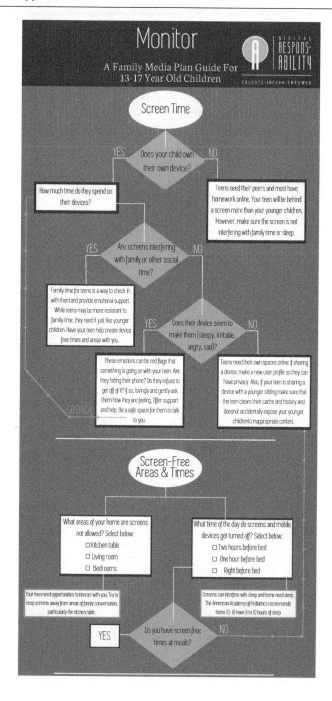

Media Consumption

When you and your child have recreational screen time you (check any of the below):

☐ Watch media with your child
☐ Play video games with your child
☐ Video chat with friends or relative
☐ Use media to be creative such as research, work on school projects, make art etc.

If none, what is one that you are or could be doing now?

Your teen is starting to look for jobs and colleges, and others are looking for them too. Encourage your teen to create content, not just consume it. Continue to play and watch media together.

Digital citizenship

Digital citizenship is the ethical and responsible use of technology. Here are some digital citizenship rules for teens: (check any of the rules you follow in your own home)

☐ Follow family rules on media
☐ When someone is talking to you, do not look at a phone or other device
☐ Tell a parent or trusted adult if you get pictures or messages that make you uncomfortable
☐ Do not share other people's information or pictures without permission
☐ Do not share your personal information online with those you don't know
☐ Being kind and not bullying online
☐ Asking permission to purchase or sell things online
☐ Do not text and drive

References:American Academy of Pediatrics (Copyright © 2016) - Council on Communications and Media Digital Citizenship: Teaching Strategies and Practice from the Field by Carrie Rogers-Whitehead

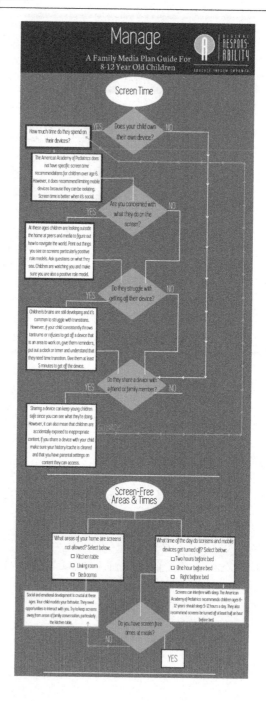

Media Consumption

What positive recreational screen time activities do you and your child have? Check any below.

☐ Play together on apps or video games
☐ Watch media together
☐ Video chat with friends and relatives

If none, what is one that you are or could be doing now?

Children learn better from media when they share the experience with an adult. Watching and playing together can help you stay connected with your child, and helps keep them safe.

Digital Citizenship

Digital citizenship is the ethical and responsible use of technology. Here are some digital citizenship rules for children these ages: (check any of the rules you follow in your own home)

☐ Follow family rules on media
☐ When someone is talking to you, do not look at a phone or other device
☐ Tell a parent or trusted adult if you get pictures or messages that make you uncomfortable
☐ Ask permission to use a caregiver or friend's device
☐ Do not share other people's information or pictures without permission
☐ Do not share your personal information online with those you don't know
☐ Do not use a phone or play a game while crossing a street
☐ Ask permission to create online accounts and share passwords with parents

References: American Academy of Pediatrics (Copyright © 2016) - Council on Communications and Media Digital Citizenship, Teaching Strategies and Practice from the Field by Carrie Rogers-Whitehead.

Resources

Chapter I

Anderson, Monica, and Jingjing Jiang. "Teens, Social Media & Technology 2018." *Pew Research Center*. Pew Research Center: Internet, Science & Tech, May 30, 2020. www.pewresearch.org/internet/2018/05/31/teens-social-media-technology-2018/#vast-majority-of-teens-have-access-to-a-home-computer-or-smartphone (Accessed May 28, 2020).

Campbell, Colin. "How to Write a Video Game Story." *Polygon*. Polygon, January 10, 2019. www.polygon.com/features/2019/1/10/18165611/how-to-write-a-video-game-story-narrative-building-tips (Accessed January 26, 2019).

Gough, Christina. "Global Consumer Spend on eSports 2020." *Statista*, April 4, 2017. www.statista.com/statistics/691794/consumer-esports-spend/ (Accessed May 21, 2020).

Gough, Christina. "U.S. Average Age of Video Gamers 2019." *Statista*, September 18, 2019. www.statista.com/statistics/189582/age-of-us-video-game-players-since-2010/ (Accessed October 10, 2018).

Hibberd, James. "If You Think 2018 Had Too Many TV Shows, Here's Why." *EW.com*. https://ew.com/tv/2018/12/13/number-tv-shows-2018/ (Accessed January 11, 2019).

"IEEE Spectrum: Technology, Engineering, and Science News." https://spectrum.ieee.org/video/telecom/wireless/everything-you-need-to-know-about-5g (Accessed January 11, 2019).

Intelligence, Business Insider. "There Will Be 24 Billion IoT Devices Installed on Earth by 2020." *Business Insider*. Business Insider, June 9, 2016. www.businessinsider.com/there-will-be-34-billion-iot-devices-installed-on-earth-by-2020-2016-5 (Accessed October 10, 2018).

"Internet Access Services Reports." *Federal Communications Commission*, September 20, 2019. www.fcc.gov/internet-access-services-reports.

Jenkins, Aric. "Spotify: Nevermind Profits." *Fortune*, May 30, 2018. http://fortune.com/2018/05/30/spotify-ipo-profit/ (Accessed January 14, 2019).

Lamont, Tom. "Napster: The Day the Music Was Set Free." *The Guardian.* Guardian News and Media, February 24, 2013. www.theguardian.com/music/2013/feb/24/napster-music-free-file-sharing (Accessed January 14, 2019).

Perez, Matt. "Report: Esports to Grow Substantially and Near Billion-Dollar Revenues in 2018." *Forbes*, February 21, 2018. www.forbes.com/sites/mattperez/2018/02/21/report-esports-to-grow-substantially-and-near-a-billion-dollar-revenues-in-2018/#dac91e52b019 (Accessed October 10, 2018).

Richter, Felix. "Infographic: The Generation Gap in Music Streaming Adoption." *Statista Infographics*, March 16, 2015. www.statista.com/chart/3313/music-streaming-generation-gap/ (Accessed January 14, 2019).

Rogers-Whitehead, Carrie. "Is WiGig the Answer to Faster WiFi?" *KSL*, November 14, 2016. www.ksl.com/?sid=42208599&nid=1012&title=is-wigig-the-answer-to-faster-wifi (Accessed October 12, 2018).

Rovell, Darren. "427 Million People Will Be Watching Esports by 2019, Reports Newzoo." *ESPN*. ESPN Internet Ventures, May 11, 2016. www.espn.com/esports/story/_/id/15508214/427-million-people-watching-esports-2019-reports-newzoo.

"The $50B Mobile Gaming Industry: Statistics, Revenue [Infographic]." *Mediakix*, July 28, 2019. http://mediakix.com/2018/03/mobile-gaming-industry-statistics-market-revenue/#gs.ipdCeKs (Accessed October 10, 2018).

Townsend, Tess. "What Bill Gates Got Wrong about the Internet in the 1990s." *Inc.com*, July 1, 2016. www.inc.com/tess-townsend/what-bill-gates-got-wrong-about-the-internet-in-the-1990s.html (Accessed January 10, 2019).

Chapter 2

Lilienfeld, Scott O. "Why 'Just Say No' Doesn't Work." *Scientific American*, January 1, 2014. www.scientificamerican.com/article/why-just-say-no-doesnt-work/ (Accessed January 14, 2020).

Petrosino, A.J., C. Turpin-Petrosino, and J.O. Finkenauer. "Well-Meaning Programs Can Have Harmful Effects: Lessons from the 'Scared Straight' Experiments." *Crime and Delinquency* 46, no. 3 (2000): 354–379.

Public Affairs. "Who Is at Risk." *StopBullying.gov,* December 4, 2019. www.stopbullying.gov/bullying/at-risk (Accessed January 14, 2020).

Rogers-Whitehead, Carrie. "What Prevention Science Tells Us about Cyberbullying." *ISTE*, June 19, 2018. www.iste.org/explore/Digital-citizenship/What-prevention-science-tells-us-about-cyberbullying (Accessed January 14, 2020).

Teen Rescue. "Teen Rescue: Texas Troubled Youth Boarding School." River View Christian Academy, June 2, 2020. www.teenrescue.com/ (Accessed March 7, 2020).

U.S. Department of Health and Human Services. *Youth Violence: A Report of the Surgeon General*. Rockville, MD: U.S. Department of Health and Human Services, Centers for Disease Control and Prevention, National Center for Injury Prevention and Control: Substance Abuse and Mental Health Services Administration, Center for Mental Health Services; and National Institutes of Health, National Institute of Mental Health. Government Printing Office, 2001.

Wang, Amy. "A Teen Checked Into an Internet-Addiction Camp in China: He Was Dead Two Days Later." *The Washington Post*. WP Company, August 14, 2017. www.washingtonpost.com/news/worldviews/wp/2017/08/14/a-teen-checked-into-an-internet-addiction-camp-in-china-he-was-dead-two-days-later/ (Accessed March 7, 2020).

"What Is SEL?" *CASEL*. https://casel.org/what-is-sel/ (Accessed May 23, 2020).

Wilkins, N., B. Tsao, M. Hertz, R. Davis, and J. Klevens. "Connecting the Dots: An Overview of the Links Among Multiple Forms of Violence." *National Center for Injury Prevention and Control*, Centers for Disease Control and Prevention, 2014. https://www.cdc.gov/violenceprevention/pdf/connecting_the_dots-a.pdf.

Chapter 3

Children

Carter, Christine Michel. "The Complete Guide to Generation Alpha, the Children of Millennials." *Forbes*, February 25, 2019. www.forbes.com/sites/christinecarter/2016/12/21/the-complete-guide-to-generation-alpha-the-children-of-millennials/#5d8bd2362363 (Accessed April 1, 2020).

Christakis, Erika. "The Dangers of Distracted Parenting." *The Atlantic*. Atlantic Media Company, June 16, 2018. www.theatlantic.com/magazine/archive/2018/07/the-dangers-of-distracted-parenting/561752/ (Accessed April 16, 2020).

"Computer Vision Syndrome: Causes, Symptoms and Treatments." *WebMD*, August 17, 2019. www.webmd.com/eye-health/computer-vision-syndrome#1 (Accessed April 1, 2020).

Dimock, Michael. "Defining Generations: Where Millennials End and Generation Z Begins." *Pew Research Center*, January 17, 2019. www.pewresearch.org/fact-tank/2019/01/17/where-millennials-end-and-generation-z-begins/ (Accessed April 1, 2020).

"Generation Alpha." *Wikipedia*. Wikimedia Foundation, June 4, 2020. https://en.wikipedia.org/wiki/Generation_Alpha (Accessed April 1, 2020).

"Home." *Ages and Stages*, May 30, 2019. https://agesandstages.com/ (Accessed April 14, 2020).

Jordan, Amy B., and Daniel Romer. *Media and the Well-Being of Children and Adolescents*. New York: Oxford University Press, 2014, 176–177.

Livingston, Gretchen. "Childlessness Falls, Family Size Grows among Highly Educated Women." *Pew Research Center's Social & Demographic Trends Project*, May 30, 2020. www.pewsocialtrends.org/2015/05/07/childlessness-falls-family-size-grows-among-highly-educated-women/ (Accessed April 1, 2020).

"The Prevalence of Peanut Allergy Has Trebled in 15 Years." *The Economist*. The Economist Newspaper, October 19, 2019. www.economist.com/graphic-detail/2019/10/03/the-prevalence-of-peanut-allergy-has-trebled-in-15-years?cid1=cust/dailypicks1/n/bl/n/2019103n/owned/n/n/dailypicks1/n/n/NA/319028/n (Accessed March 27, 2020).

"Understanding Generation Alpha: The Most Diverse Generation Yet." *Hotwire*. www.hotwireglobal.com/feature/genalpha3 (Accessed April 1, 2020).

Media and Popular Culture

Alli, Renee A. "Emotional Development in Preschoolers: From Age 3 to 5." *WebMD*, October 22, 2018. www.webmd.com/parenting/preschooler-emotional-development#1 (Accessed April 14, 2020).

Ashby, Emily. "Parent Reviews for PAW Patrol: Common Sense Media." *Common Sense Media*. Common Sense Media: Ratings, Reviews, and Advice, August 8, 2013. www.commonsensemedia.org/tv-reviews/paw-patrol/user-reviews/adult (Accessed April 19, 2020).

Barr, R. "Transfer of Learning between 2D and 3D Sources during Infancy: Informing Theory and Practice." *Developmental Review: DR* 30, no. 2 (2010): 128–154. https://doi.org/10.1016/j.dr.2010.03.001.

boyd, danah. *It's Complicated: The Social Lives of Networked Teens*. New Haven: Yale University Press, 2015.

Campbell, Olivia. "Why Gender Stereotypes in Kids' Shows Are a Really Big Deal." *Kids TV Shows Gender Stereotypes*. Toxic Masculinity, December 5, 2017. www.refinery29.com/en-us/kids-shows-gender-roles-stereotypes (Accessed April 19, 2020).

"CDC's Developmental Milestones." *Centers for Disease Control and Prevention*. Centers for Disease Control and Prevention, December 5, 2019. www.cdc.gov/ncbddd/actearly/milestones/index.html (Accessed April 14, 2020).

Cohen, Kristin. "YouTube Channel Owners: Is Your Content Directed to Children?" *Federal Trade Commission*, November 22, 2019. www.ftc.gov/news-events/blogs/business-blog/2019/11/youtube-channel-owners-your-content-directed-children (Accessed April 17, 2020).

"Demographics of Social Media Users and Adoption in the United States." *Pew Research Center*. Pew Research Center: Internet, Science & Tech, June 12, 2019. www.pewresearch.org/internet/fact-sheet/social-media/ (Accessed April 17, 2020).

"Early Brain Development and Health." *Centers for Disease Control and Prevention*. Centers for Disease Control and Prevention, March 5, 2020. www.cdc.gov/ncbddd/childdevelopment/early-brain-development.html (Accessed April 14, 2020).

Ellis, Emma Grey. "Marketers Wanted a New Generation to Target, Hence Alphas." *Wired*. Conde Nast, September, 17, 2019. www.wired.com/story/marketing-generation-alpha/ (Accessed April 17, 2020).

Guernsey, Lisa. "The Genius of 'Baby Einstein'." *The New York Times*, August 16, 2007. www.nytimes.com/2007/08/16/opinion/16guernsey.html (Accessed April 16, 2020).

Knorr, Caroline. "Gender Stereotypes Are Messing with Your Kid." *Common Sense Media*. Common Sense Media: Ratings, Reviews, and Advice, June 19, 2017. www.commonsensemedia.org/blog/gender-stereotypes-are-messing-with-your-kid (Accessed April 19, 2020).

Moser, Alecia, Laura Zimmermann, Kelly Dickerson, Amanda Grenell, Rachel Barr, and Peter Gerhardstein. "They Can Interact, But Can They Learn? Toddlers' Transfer Learning from Touchscreens and Television." *Journal of Experimental Child Psychology* 137(2015): 137–155. doi:10.1016/j.jecp.2015.04.002.

Nguyen, Tay. "GDPR Matchup: The Children's Online Privacy Protection Act." *International Association of Privacy Professionals*. GDPR Matchup: The Children's Online Privacy Protection Act, May 6, 2020. https://iapp.org/news/a/gdpr-matchup-the-childrens-online-privacy-protection-act/ (Accessed April 17, 2020).

Perez, Sarah. "Family-Friendly Spotify Kids App Launches in the U.S., Canada and France." *TechCrunch*, March 31, 2020. https://techcrunch.com/2020/03/31/family-friendly-spotify-kids-app-launches-in-the-u-s-canada-and-france/ (Accessed April 17, 2020).

Radesky, J., A.L. Miller, K.L. Rosenblum, D. Appugliese, N. Kaciroti, and J.C. Lumeng. "Maternal Mobile Device Use during a Structured Parent-Child Interaction Task." *Academic Pediatrics* 15, no. 2 (2015): 238–244. https://doi.org/10.1016/j.acap.2014.10.001.

Siegel, Rachel. "Tweens, Teens and Screens: The Average Time Kids Spend Watching Online Videos Has Doubled in 4 Years." *The Washington Post*. WP Company, October 29, 2019. www.washingtonpost.com/technology/2019/10/29/survey-average-time-young-people-spend-watching-videos-mostly-youtube-has-doubled-since/ (Accessed April 17, 2020).

"YouTube by the Numbers: Stats, Demographics & Fun Facts." *Omnicore*, February 10, 2020. www.omnicoreagency.com/youtube-statistics/ (Accessed April 17, 2020).

Chapter 4

"Age Appropriate Info on Puberty for Tweens and Their Parents." *Amaze.* https://amaze.org/ (Accessed April 3, 2020).

Auxier, Brooke, and Monica Anderson. "As Schools Close Due to the Coronavirus, Some U.S. Students Face a Digital 'Homework Gap'." *Pew Research Center*, March 16, 2020. www.pewresearch.org/fact-tank/2020/03/16/as-schools-close-due-to-the-coronavirus-some-u-s-students-face-a-digital-homework-gap/ (Accessed March 23, 2020).

"Eight-in-Ten Blacks Say Social Media Help Shed Light on Rarely Discussed Issues: The Same Share of Whites Say These Sites Distract from More Important Issues." *Pew Research Center.* Pew Research Center: Internet, Science & Tech, July 10, 2018. www.pewresearch.org/internet/2018/07/11/public-attitudes-toward-political-engagement-on-social-media/pi_2018-07-10_social-activism_0-20/ (Accessed March 25, 2020).

Gough, Christina. "Fortnite Popularity among Children in the U.S. 2018." *Statista*, December 3, 2019. www.statista.com/statistics/985792/fortnite-playing-children-united-states/ (Accessed March 23, 2020).

Hussain, Tamoor. "Nintendo Switch Digital Game File Sizes Revealed." *GameSpot*, February 20, 2017. www.gamespot.com/articles/nintendo-switch-digital-game-file-sizes-revealed/1100-6448026/ (Accessed March 26, 2020).

"Instagram Help Center." Controlling Your Visibility | Instagram Help Center. https://help.instagram.com/116024195217477/ (Accessed March 25, 2020).

"The Legend of Zelda." *Wikipedia.* Wikimedia Foundation, June 5, 2020. https://en.wikipedia.org/wiki/The_Legend_of_Zelda (Accessed March 26, 2020).

Mann, Mali. "Puberty, Adolescence, and Shame." In *Shame.* London: Routledge, 2016. https://doi.org/10.4324/9780429480089.

"Media Use by Tweens and Teens 2019: Infographic: Common Sense Media." Common Sense Media: Ratings, Reviews, and Advice. www.commonsensemedia.org/Media-use-by-tweens-and-teens-2019-infographic (Accessed March 17, 2020).

Miranda, Cristina. "What to Ask before Buying Internet-Connected Toys." *Consumer Information*, December 9, 2019. www.consumer.ftc.gov/blog/2019/12/what-ask-buying-internet-connected-toys (Accessed March 25, 2020).

Perez, Sarah. "Messenger Kids Adds Expanded Parental Controls, Details How Much Kids' Data Facebook Collects." *TechCrunch*, February 4, 2020. https://techcrunch.com/2020/02/04/messenger-kids-adds-expanded-parental-controls-details-how-much-kids-data-facebook-collects/ (Accessed March 25, 2020).

Perrin, Andrew, and Monica Anderson. "Share of U.S. Adults Using Social Media, Including Facebook, Is Mostly Unchanged since 2018."

Pew Research Center, April 10, 2019. www.pewresearch.org/fact-tank/ 2019/04/10/share-of-u-s-adults-using-social-media-including-facebook-is-mostly-unchanged-since-2018/ (Accessed March 23, 2020).

Planned Parenthood. "Puberty in Females and Males: Get Facts and Info about Puberty." *Planned Parenthood*. www.plannedparenthood.org/ learn/teens/puberty (Accessed March 8, 2020).

Rogers-Whitehead, Carrie. "Educators: Help Parents Talk to Their Kids about Tech." *ISTE*, February 25, 2020. www.iste.org/explore/educators-help-parents-talk-their-kids-about-tech (Accessed March 26, 2020).

Shipman, Claire, and Katty Kay. "How Puberty Kills Girls' Confidence." *The Atlantic*. Atlantic Media Company, September 21, 2018. www.the atlantic.com/family/archive/2018/09/puberty-girls-confidence/563804/ (Accessed March 23, 2020).

Steinberg, L., and K.C. Monahan. "Age Differences in Resistance to Peer Influence." *Developmental Psychology* 43, no. 6 (2007): 1531–1543.

Chapter 5

Anastassiou, Andrea. "Sexting and Young People: A Review of the Qualitative Literature." *Qualitative Report* 22 (2017): 8–16.

Booker, C.L., Y.J. Kelly, and A. Sacker. "Gender Differences in the Associations between Age Trends of Social Media Interaction and Well-Being among 10–15 Year Olds in the UK." *BMC Public Health* 18, no. 321 (2018). https://doi.org/10.1186/s12889-018-5220-4.

"Child Sex Trafficking Statistics." *Thorn*, January 17, 2020. www.thorn. org/child-trafficking-statistics/ (Accessed March 31, 2020).

CitizenScience.gov. www.citizenscience.gov/ (Accessed April 13, 2020).

Driver, Saige. "Social Media Screenings Gain in Popularity." *Business News Daily*, October 7, 2018. www.businessnewsdaily.com/2377-social-media-hiring.html (Accessed April 13, 2020).

Guldi, Melanie, and Chris M. Herbst. "Offline Effects of Online Connecting: The Impact of Broadband Diffusion on Teen Fertility Decisions." *Journal of Population Economics* 30 no. 1 (2016): 69–91. https://doi. org/10.1007/s00148-016-0605-0.

Hinduja, Sameer. "It Is Time to Teach Safe Sexting." *Cyberbullying Research Center*, January 16, 2020. https://cyberbullying.org/it-is-time-to-teach-safe-sexting (Accessed April 6, 2020).

https://en.wikipedia.org/wiki/Pornhub (Accessed April 5, 2020).

Leonhardt, Nathan D., Brian J. Willoughby, and Bonnie Young-Petersen. "Damaged Goods: Perception of Pornography Addiction as a Mediator between Religiosity and Relationship Anxiety Surrounding Pornography Use." *The Journal of Sex Research* 55, no. 3 (2017): 357–368. https://doi. org/10.1080/00224499.2017.1295013.

Lindberg, Laura Duberstein, Isaac Maddow-Zimet, and Heather Boonstra. "Changes in Adolescents' Receipt of Sex Education, 2006–2013."

Journal of Adolescent Health 58, no. 6 (2016): 621–627. https://doi.org/10.1016/j.jadohealth.2016.02.004.

Livingstone, Sonia, Leslie Haddon, Anke Görzig, and Kjartan Ólafsson. "Risks and Safety on the Internet: The Perspective of European Children: Full Findings and Policy Implications from the EU Kids Online Survey of 9–16 Year Olds and Their Parents in 25 Countries." *EU Kids Online*, Deliverable D4, EU Kids Online Network, London, UK, 2011.

Madigan, Sheri, and Gina Dimitropoulos. "One in Five Youth See Unwanted Sexual Content Online, Says New Research." *The Conversation*, March 26, 2020. https://theconversation.com/one-in-five-youth-see-unwanted-sexual-content-online-says-new-research-96097 (Accessed March 31, 2020).

Madigan, Sheri, Vanessa Villani, Corry Azzopardi, Danae Laut, Tanya Smith, Jeff R. Temple, Dillon Browne, and Gina Dimitropoulos. "The Prevalence of Unwanted Online Sexual Exposure and Solicitation Among Youth: A Meta-Analysis." *Journal of Adolescent Health* 63, no. 2 (2018): 133–141. https://doi.org/10.1016/j.jadohealth.2018.03.012.

Marston and Lewis. "Anal Heterosex among Young People and Implications for Health Promotion: A Qualitative Study from the UK. *BMJ Open* 4 (2014): 1–7. doi:10.1136/bmjopen-2014-004996.

Marston, Cicely and Lewis, Ruth. "Anal Heterosex among Young People and Implications for Health Promotion: A Qualitative Study from the UK. *BMJ Open* 4 (2014): 1–7. doi:10.1136/bmjopen-2014-004996.

Morin, Amy. "The Developmental Milestones 18-Year-Olds Reach." *Verywell Family*, July 15, 2019. www.verywellfamily.com/18-year-old-developmental-milestones-2609030 (Accessed March 29, 2020).

National Research Council (US) and Institute of Medicine (US) Forum on Adolescence, and Kipke. MD, editor. *Adolescent Development and the Biology of Puberty: Summary of a Workshop on New Research.* Washington, DC: National Academies Press (US), 1999. Adolescent Development and the Biology of Puberty. www.ncbi.nlm.nih.gov/books/NBK224692/.

Pate, Deanna. "The Skills Companies Need Most in 2020 and How to Learn Them." *LinkedIn Learning.* https://learning.linkedin.com/blog/top-skills/the-skills-companies-need-most-in-2020-and-how-to-learn-them (Accessed April 13, 2020).

Peter, J., and P.M. Valkenburg. "Adolescents and Pornography: A Review of 20 Years of Research." *The Journal of Sex Research* 53, no. 4–5 (2016): 209–531.

Planned Parenthood. "State of Sex Education in USA: Health Education in Schools." *Planned Parenthood.* www.plannedparenthood.org/learn/for-educators/whats-state-sex-education-us (Accessed April 5, 2020).

Roose, Kevin. "This Was the Alt-Right's Favorite Chat App. Then Came Charlottesville." *The New York Times*, August 15, 2017. www.nytimes.com/2017/08/15/technology/discord-chat-app-alt-right.html (Accessed April 10, 2020).

Rothman, Emily F., Nicole Daley, and Jess Alder. "A Pornography Literacy Program for Adolescents." *American Journal of Public Health* 110, no. 2 (February 1, 2020): 154–156. https://doi.org/10.2105/AJPH.2019.305468.

Shroff, Amita. "Puberty and Girls: What to Expect When Girls Hit Puberty." *WebMD*, April 23, 2018. https://teens.webmd.com/girls/facts-about-puberty-girls (Accessed March 29, 2020).

"Social Media, Social Life Infographic: Common Sense Media." Common Sense Media: Ratings, Reviews, and Advice. www.commonsensemedia.org/social-media-social-life-infographic (Accessed April 8, 2020).

U.S. Department of Health and Human Services, Administration for Children, Youth and Families. *Guidance to States and Services on Addressing Human Trafficking of Children and Youth in the United States.* Washington, DC: Author, 2014. www.acf.hhs.gov/sites/default/files/cb/acyf_human_trafficking_guidance.pdf.

Varner, J., K. Hoch, M.C. Goates, and C. Hanson. "Proactive Protection for Adolescents, the Innocent Victim: Risk and Protective Factors for Pornography." Presentation at *the Utah Society of Public Health Educators Annual Conference*, Ogden, UT, September, 2017.

Wolak, Janis, David Finkelhor, Wendy Walsh, and Leah Treitman. "Sextortion of Minors: Characteristics and Dynamics." *Journal of Adolescent Health* 62, no. 1 (2018): 72–79. https://doi.org/10.1016/j.jadohealth.2017.08.014.

Zaloom, Shafia. *Sex, Teens, and Everything in between: The New and Necessary Conversations Today's Teenagers Need to Have about Consent, Sexual Harassment, Healthy Relationships, Love and More.* Naperville, IL: Sourcebooks, 2019.

Chapter 6

Barrett, Lisa. *How Emotions Are Made: The Secret Life of the Brain.* New York: Mariner Books, 2018.

Ghekiere, A., J. Van Cauwenberg, A. Vandendriessche, et al. "Trends in Sleeping Difficulties among European Adolescents: Are These Associated with Physical Inactivity and Excessive Screen Time?" *International Journal of Public Health* 64 (2019): 487–498. https://doi.org/10.1007/s00038-018-1188-1.

Keith, Emma. "Norman Parents Express Concerns with School Technology Use at Board Meeting." *Norman Transcript*, January 14, 2020. www.normantranscript.com/news/education/norman-parents-express-concerns-with-school-technology-use-at-board-meeting/article_e3c7c87a-8a9a-5916-b5c7-06e3086c55a2.html (Accessed May 17, 2020).

Odgers, Candice L., and Michaeline R. Jensen. "Annual Research Review: Adolescent Mental Health in the Digital Age: Facts, Fears, and Future Directions." *Journal of Child Psychology and Psychiatry* 61, no. 3 (2020): 336–348. https://doi.org/10.1111/jcpp.13190.

Popper, Nathaniel. "Panicking about Your Kids' Phones? New Research Says Don't." *The New York Times*, January 17, 2020. www.nytimes.com/2020/01/17/technology/kids-smartphones-depression.html?algo=identity (Accessed April 4, 2020).

"Sleep for Teenagers." *Sleep Foundation*, June 1, 2020. www.sleepfoundation.org/articles/teens-and-sleep (Accessed May 19, 2020).

Truong, Debbie. "More Students Are Learning on Laptops and Tablets in Class: Some Parents Want to Hit the Off Switch." *The Washington Post*. WP Company, February 1, 2020. www.washingtonpost.com/local/education/more-students-are-learning-on-laptops-and-tablets-in-class-some-parents-want-to-hit-the-off-switch/2020/02/01/d53134d0-db1e-11e9-a688–303693fb4b0b_story.html (Accessed May 17, 2020).

Twenge, Jean. "Have Smartphones Destroyed a Generation?" *The Atlantic*. Atlantic Media Company, September, 2017. www.theatlantic.com/magazine/archive/2017/09/has-the-smartphone-destroyed-a-generation/534198/ (Accessed May 14, 2020).

Walker, Matthew. *Why We Sleep: Unlocking the Power of Sleep and Dreams*. Scribner: New York, 2018.

Yoo, Seung-Schik, Ninad Gujar, Peter Hu, Ferenc A. Jolesz, and Matthew P. Walker. "The Human Emotional Brain without Sleep: A Prefrontal Amygdala Disconnect." *Current Biology* 17, no. 20 (2007). https://doi.org/10.1016/j.cub.2007.08.007.

Sleep and Screentime Research

Guerrero, Michelle D., Joel D. Barnes, Jean-Philippe Chaput, and Mark S. Tremblay. "Screen Time and Problem Behaviors in Children: Exploring the Mediating Role of Sleep Duration." *The International Journal of Behavioral Nutrition and Physical Activity*. BioMed Central, November 14, 2019. www.ncbi.nlm.nih.gov/pmc/articles/PMC6854622/ (Accessed April 27, 2020).

"Mindfulness Meditation: A Research-Proven Way to Reduce Stress." American Psychological Association (APA), October 30, 2019. www.apa.org/topics/mindfulness-meditation (Accessed May 19, 2020).

Rogers-Whitehead, Carrie. "5 Tips to Help Your Kid Put Down the Screen and Go to Sleep." *KSL.com*. May 3, 2018. www.ksl.com/article/46313498/5-tips-to-help-your-kid-put-down-the-screen-and-go-to-sleep (Accessed May 19, 2020).

Chapter 7

"APA Reaffirms Position on Violent Video Games and Violent Behavior." *American Psychological Association*. www.apa.org/news/press/releases/2020/03/violent-video-games-behavior (Accessed April 28, 2020).

Arena, D. "Video Games as Tillers of Soil." *Theory Into Practice* 54, no. 2 (2015): 94–100. https://doi.org/10.1080/00405841.2015.1010843.

"Childhood Obesity Facts." *Centers for Disease Control and Prevention*, June 24, 2019. www.cdc.gov/obesity/data/childhood.html (Accessed April 23, 2020).

Cooper, J., and D. Mackie. "Video Games and Aggression in Children." *Journal of Applied Social Psychology* 16 (1986): 726–744.

Entin, Esther. "All Work and No Play: Why Your Kids Are More Anxious . . ." *The Atlantic*, October 21, 2011. www.theatlantic.com/health/archive/2011/10/all-work-and-no-play-why-your-kids-are-more-anxious-depressed/246422/ (Accessed April 23, 2020).

"Gaming Disorder." *World Health Organization*. www.who.int/newsroom/q-a-detail/gaming-disorder (Accessed April 21, 2020).

Gonzalez, Oscar. "Fortnite Made $1.8 Billion Last Year, But It's Still a Game in Decline." *CNET*, February 22, 2020. www.cnet.com/news/fortnite-made-1-8-billion-last-year-but-its-still-a-game-in-decline/ (Accessed April 27, 2020).

"Home." *ESRB Ratings*. www.esrb.org/ (Accessed April 28, 2020).

Jamruk, K. "The Weight Game: Fighting Childhood Obesity with Childhood Video Technology." *Journal of Legal Medicine* 37, no. 1/2 (2017): 175–194. https://doi.org/10.1080/01947648.2017.1303409.

Jeong, E.J., C.J. Ferguson, and S.J. Lee. "Pathological Gaming in Young Adolescents: A Longitudinal Study Focused on Academic Stress and Self-Control in South Korea." *Journal of Youth and Adolescence* 48, no. 12 (2019): 2333–2342.

Ke, Fengfeng, and Jewoong Moon. "Virtual Collaborative Gaming as Social Skills Training for High-Functioning Autistic Children." *British Journal of Educational Technology* 49, no. 4 (2018): 728–741. https://doi.org/10.1111/bjet.12626. https://en.wikipedia.org/wiki/Half-Life:_Alyx (Accessed April 21, 2020).

Kenney, Erica L., and Steven L. Gortmaker. "United States Adolescents' Television, Computer, Videogame, Smartphone, and Tablet Use: Associations with Sugary Drinks, Sleep, Physical Activity, and Obesity." *The Journal of Pediatrics* 182 (2017): 144–149. https://doi.org/10.1016/j.jpeds.2016.11.015.

Kim, Daum. "Horses to the Rescue of Korea's Internet-Addicted Teens." *Reuters*, January 9, 2013. www.reuters.com/article/us-korea-internet-horses/horses-to-the-rescue-of-koreas-internet-addicted-teens-idUSBRE90803020130109 (Accessed April 21, 2020).

Kim, Victoria. "He Played for 72 Hours Straight: South Korea Wrestles with Video Game Addiction." *Los Angeles Times*, October 17, 2019. www.latimes.com/world-nation/story/2019-10-17/south-korea-video-game-addiction-mental-health (Accessed April 21, 2020).

Markey, Patrick M., and Christopher J. Ferguson. *Moral Combat: Why the War on Violent Video Games Is Wrong*. Dallas, TX: BenBella Books, 2017.

"Massively Multiplayer Online Role-Playing Game." *Wikipedia*. Wikimedia Foundation, June 14, 2020. https://en.wikipedia.org/wiki/Massively_multiplayer_online_role-playing_game (Accessed April 26, 2020).

Mayer, Richard E. *Multimedia Learning*. Cambridge University Press, 2001.

Muncy, Julie. "Depression and the Solace of 'Grinding' in Online Games." *Wired*. Conde Nast, July 24, 2019. www.wired.com/story/videogame-grinding-depression/ (Accessed April 26, 2020).

Patchin, Justin W. "Are 'Gamers' More Likely to Be 'Bullies'?" *Cyberbullying Research Center*, September 21, 2018. https://cyberbullying.org/are-gamers-more-likely-to-be-bullies (Accessed April 28, 2020).

Publisher. "An Official** Division 46 Statement on the WHO Proposal to Include Gaming Related Disorders in ICD-11." *The Amplifier Magazine*, June 21, 2018. https://div46amplifier.com/2018/06/21/an-official-division-46-statement-on-the-who-proposal-to-include-gaming-related-disorders-in-icd-11/v (Accessed April 17, 2020).

"Resolution on Violence in Video Games and Interactive Media." *American Psychological Association*, 2005. www.apa.org/about/policy/interactive-media.pdf (Accessed April 28, 2020).

Robinson, Thomas N., Jorge A. Banda, Lauren Hale, Amy Shirong Lu, Frances Fleming-Milici, Sandra L. Calvert, and Ellen Wartella. "Screen Media Exposure and Obesity in Children and Adolescents." *Pediatrics* 140, no. Supplement 2 (2017). https://doi.org/10.1542/peds.2016-1758k.

Rogers-Whitehead, Carrie. "The Discord with Discord: What Parents Need to Know about the Popular Gamer Chat." *KSL.com*, December 5, 2018. www.ksl.com/article/46441334/the-discord-with-discord-what-parents-need-to-know-about-the-popular-gamer-chat (Accessed April 28, 2020).

Rogers-Whitehead, Carrie. "Loot Boxes: What Parents Need to Know about the Controversial Video Game Craze." *KSL.com*, March 12, 2019. www.ksl.com/article/46509686/loot-boxes-what-parents-need-to-know-about-the-controversial-video-game-craze (Accessed April 27, 2020).

Stanford University. "Virtual Reality Can Help Make People More Empathetic." *Stanford News*, October 16, 2018. https://news.stanford.edu/2018/10/17/virtual-reality-can-help-make-people-empathetic (Accessed December 11, 2019).

Stiller, Anja, Jan Weber, Finja Strube, and Thomas Mößle. "Caregiver Reports of Screen Time Use of Children with Autism Spectrum Disorder: A Qualitative Study." *Behavioral Sciences* 9, no. 5 (2019): 56. https://doi.org/10.3390/bs9050056.

Watson, Amy. "U.S. Media Usage: Time Spent Watching Television 2021." *Statista*, September 11, 2019. www.statista.com/statistics/186833/average-television-use-per-person-in-the-us-since-2002/ (Accessed April 28, 2020).

Wikipedia. "Half Life Alyx" (Accessed April 21, 2020)

Chapter 8

"About the International Age Rating Coalition: IARC." About the International Age Rating Coalition | IARC. www.globalratings.com/about.aspx (Accessed May 5, 2020).

"Advertising and Marketing | Federal Trade Commission." *Federal Trade Commission*. www.ftc.gov/tips-advice/business-center/advertising-and-marketing (Accessed May 5, 2020).

"Digital Media Projected to Capture 60.1% Share of PreK-12 Instructional Materials in 2019." *Simba Information*. www.simbainformation.com/Content/Blog/2019/08/08/Digital-Media-Projected-to-Capture-601-Share-of-PreK-12-Instructional-Materials-in-2019 (Accessed May 11, 2020).

"DisneyNow." *Disneynow.go.com*. https://disneynow.com/apps (Accessed May 5, 2020).

Guerrero, Michelle D., Joel D. Barnes, Jean-Philippe Chaput, and Mark S. Tremblay. "Screen Time and Problem Behaviors in Children: Exploring the Mediating Role of Sleep Duration." *The International Journal of Behavioral Nutrition and Physical Activity*. BioMed Central, November 14, 2019. www.ncbi.nlm.nih.gov/pmc/articles/PMC6854622/ (Accessed April 17, 2020).

Helyn, Kim, Esther Care, and Alvin Vista. "Education Systems Need Alignment for Teaching and Learning 21st Century Skills." *Brookings*, January 30, 2019. www.brookings.edu/blog/education-plus-development/2019/01/30/education-systems-need-alignment-for-teaching-and-learning-21st-century-skills/ (Accessed May 13, 2020).

Herold, Benjamin. "COPPA and Schools: The (Other) Federal Student Privacy Law, Explained." *Education Week*, October 12, 2018. www.edweek.org/ew/issues/childrens-online-privacy-protection-act-coppa/index.html (Accessed May 5, 2020).

Kievlan, Patricia Monticello. "Kid Reviews for Amino-Communities, Chat, Forums, and Groups: Common Sense Media." *Common Sense Media*. Common Sense Media: Ratings, Reviews, and Advice, August 1, 2016. www.commonsensemedia.org/app-reviews/amino-communities-chat-forums-and-groups/user-reviews/child (Accessed May 8, 2020).

"Learning." *YouTube*. www.youtube.com/channel/UCtFRv9O2AHqOZjjynzrv-xg/about (Accessed May 5, 2020).

Mandel, Lev L., Stella Aguinaga Bialous, and Stanton A. Glantz. "Avoiding 'Truth': Tobacco Industry Promotion of Life Skills Training." *Journal of Adolescent Health* 39, no. 6 (2006): 868–879. https://doi.org/10.1016/j.jadohealth.2006.06.010.

"Map: Coronavirus and School Closures." *Education Week*, March 6, 2020. www.edweek.org/ew/section/multimedia/map-coronavirus-and-school-closures.html (Accessed May 10, 2020).

Media Literacy
www.tandfonline.com/doi/full/10.1080/10584609.2018.1526238.

Advertising in Young Children's Apps: A Content Analysis
Meyer, Marisa, Victoria Adkins, Nalingna Yuan, Heidi M. Weeks, Yung-Ju Chang, and Jenny MD Radesky. "Author Information." *Journal of Developmental & Behavioral Pediatrics* 40, no. 1 (January 2019): 32–39. doi:10.1097/DBP.0000000000000622.

Poon, Linda. "Coronavirus Exposes How Bad America's Homework Gap Really Is." *CityLab*, March 22, 2020. www.citylab.com/equity/2020/03/coronavirus-online-schools-homework-internet-access-homework/608116/ (Accessed May 10, 2020).

Pusey, Stacey. "Digital Instructional Materials, OER Rising in PreK-12 Classrooms." *EdScoop*, October 4, 2019. https://edscoop.com/digital-instructional-materials-oer-rising-in-prek-12-classrooms/ (Accessed May 11, 2020).

Stainburn, Samantha. "High Schools Assign 3.5 Hours of Homework a Night, Survey Estimates." *Education Week: Time and Learning*, February 28, 2014. http://blogs.edweek.org/edweek/time_and_learning/2014/02/high_schools_assign_3.5_hours.html (Accessed May 10, 2020).

Yoon, Sunkyung, Mary Kleinman, Jessica Mertz, and Michael Brannick. "Is Social Network Site Usage Related to Depression? A Meta-Analysis of Facebook: Depression Relations." *Journal of Affective Disorders* 248 (2019): 65–72. https://doi.org/10.1016/j.jad.2019.01.026.

"Truth in Advertising." *Federal Trade Commission*, May 7, 2020. www.ftc.gov/news-events/media-resources/truth-advertising (Accessed May 8, 2020).

Index

4chan 82
5G Technology 10

adolescents 4, 20, 32, 65–68, 72–73, 77, 81, 83–84, 90–91, 96–97, 99, 103–104, 106, 115, 158, 161; *see also* teens
affiliate marketing 163
alarms 105; *see also* timers
Amaze.org 46–47
American Academy of Pediatrics (AAP): affecting research 98; screen time recommendations 31–32; and social media 96–97
American Psychological Association (APA) 106, 116, 129
Animal Crossing 9, 124
apps: definition 4–5; educational 143–145, 158, 161; growth of 5; history of 4
autism spectrum disorder (ASD) 118–119

babies 31; *see also* infants
boundaries 49, 56–58, 66; *see also* setting boundaries with children
British Broadcasting Corporation (BBC) 151–152
bullying 62, 130, 132; *see also* cyberbullying

Children's Online Privacy Protection Act (COPPA) 35–36, 155
Club Penguin 149–150

college and career readiness 85–87, 160
Columbine shootings 128
context: definition of 36; and gaming 137–138; and pornography 81, 83; for young children 36–37
COVID-19: changes with 149; and discord 83; and remote learning 101, 154–155; and TikTok 160
cyberbullying: and gaming 130–131; risk and protective factors 16, 22; and screen time 109; and sleep 103

D.A.R.E.: Drug Abuse Resistance Education 18–19, 21
developmental stages 27, 144; *see also* youth developmental stages
digital divide 51, 154–155
discord: and alt-right 82–83, 131; and cyberbullying 131; definition of 82; growth of 83; parental controls 132; and trolling 131–132
Disney 151, 158
Disney Junior 151, 158; *see also* Disney
doxing 132

Entertainment Software Ratings Board (ESRB): descriptors of ratings 145–146; and gaming

130, 138–139; history of 127, 145; pros and cons 164–165
eSports 9–10
exergames 121–122

Facebook: "Facebook depression" 96–97; Messenger 55, 63; Messenger Kids 35; parent communities 164; popularity 51; purchasing 55; ratings 54
family media plan 40, 170–175
farming 122, 137; see also grinding
Federal Communications Commission (FCC) 99
Federal Trade Commission (FTC): and loot boxes 125; marketing to children regulations 148; and online privacy 35–36, 155–156; recommendations on smart toys 54
filtering Internet 12, 36, 53, 150
financial literacy 161
Fortnite: all-ages community 149; grinding 122; microtransactions 123–124; popularity of 50–51, 164; settings 127, 150
freemium games 126; see also free-to-play games
free-to-play games 122, 126

gaming addiction 19, 115, 116, 140; see also video gaming addiction (VGA)
gender stereotypes: in children's media 37–38; in pornography 74
General Data Protection Regulation (GDPR) 35
Generation Alphas: definition of 25; market for 35; parents of 26; tech trends for 33; traits of 25–26; and YouTube 34–35, 159
Gen X 2
Gen Z 2, 5, 11, 33, 159, 161
Grand Theft Auto (GTA) 127, 130
grinding 122–123

hashtags 164
history of the Internet 2–3
history of videogaming 8–9, 57, 126

homework: digital materials 153; growth in 152–153; and screen time 100–101; suggestions for parents 101–102, 153–154

infants 27–28, 147
Instagram: and advertising 163; age recommendations 54; and Hispanic users 51; purchasing 55; settings 55; and social comparison 83
International Age Rating Coalition (IARC) 147
Internet of Things (IoT) 10, 53–54
Internet or gaming addiction boot camps 19–20, 115
iPhone 4

language development in young children 31–33
lateral reading 163
Legend of Zelda 57
LGBTQ+ youth 62, 71, 76
LinkedIn 85–86, 88, 160
loot boxes: criticism of 124–125; definition of 124; types of 124

marketing to children: in gaming 126; online 147
Massively Multiplayer Online Role-Playing Games 122
meditation 106–107; see also mindfulness
Messenger 35, 55, 63; see also Facebook
microtransactions: defense of 126; definition of 123; how to limit or prevent 126–127
Millennials: marketing of 147; parenting Generation Alphas 25, 35; technology of 2–3
mindfulness: apps for 107–108, 157; definition of 106; research 106–107
Minecraft 58, 135, 150
MMORPGs see Massively Multiplayer Online Role-Playing Games
mood tracking 161

Napster 6–7
narrative parenting 40–41
National Public Radio (NPR)
    151–152
newborns 27
Nickelodeon 151, 158
Nick Jr. see Nickelodeon
norms: definition of 39; gaming
    norms 136–139; for sleep
    106–106; technology norms for
    families 39–40

obesity 119–120
online privacy 35, 87, 97, 155;
    see also privacy
online support groups: for parents
    163–164; for teens 63

Paw Patrol 37–38, 151
Pinterest 51
Pokémon Go 34, 121–122
pornography: and boys 73–74; and
    gender stereotypes 74; Hentai
    76; and queer bodies 76; risk
    and protective factors 73; and
    sex education 75, 77–78; and
    shame 77; statistics 73
preschoolers 29–30
prevention science: definition of
    15–16; prevention programs
    that don't work 18–21; risk
    and protective factors definition
    16; risk and protective factors
    for pornography 73; risk and
    protective factors with peers 63;
    risk factors for digital behaviors
    21–22; risk factors for sexting
    70; and screen time 99–100;
    and smartphones 96; and social
    emotional learning 16
privacy: children's online privacy
    54, 143, 150; law 35, 155; and
    social media 56; and tracking 97
puberty: and adolescents 64–65;
    advice for parents 47; hormones
    46; physical changes 46–47; and
    shame 48; social changes 47–49;
    and tweens 31, 152

Public Broadcasting Service (PBS)
    32, 144, 151
public information on social
    media 56

ratings 138, 143, 145–147, 164;
    see also Entertainment Software
    Rating Board (ESRB)
Reddit 82
red flag behaviors 84–85
Red Pill movement 81–82
research methodology see self-
    reporting in research
Roblox: chat function 55, 157;
    definition of 157; parent
    community 164; pros and cons
    157; purchasing 55, 157
rules 2, 27, 30, 31, 39, 40, 49, 53,
    95, 106, 110, 130, 136–137;
    see also norms

Scared Straight 19, 21
screen time: concerns with 109;
    and homework 100–101;
    panic around 94–95; parenting
    strategies 110–111; and
    prevention science 99–100;
    research 95–100; and sleep
    102–106; tracking 97
self-regulation: and brain
    development 58; and gaming
    18; and sleep 104; and social
    emotional learning 17
self-reporting in research 97–98, 127
setting boundaries with children
    57–58
sex education 75–76, 161
sexting: definition of 67; growth
    of 68; and the law 70–71;
    in the media 67–68; positives
    of 68; reasons for 68–70; safe
    sexting 72
sex trafficking 71–72
sexual development 65–66
sleep: blue light 103; effects of
    screens 102–104; and mental
    health 103–104; strategies for
    improving 105; and teens 65

smartphones: alternatives to 53; growth of 4; history of 4; and mental health 96

Snapchat: age recommendations 51; profiles 56; rating 146; and tweens 51, 54

social comparison 81, 83

social emotional learning (SEL): definition of 15–16; effects of 16

social media: digital brand 88; and mental health 79–80, 99

Spotify 7

Stardew Valley 137–138

Steam 8

STEM (Science, Technology, Engineering and Math) 87

teens: mental health 77–81; and puberty 64–65; sexual maturity 66; and sleep 65, 104; talking to 90

television: and gaming 133; growth of 6; history of 5; and obesity 121; and tweens 51

Terraria 133–134

texting 2

TikTok 51, 148, 160

time management 161

timers 58, 105, 153

toddlers 28–29, 47, 147

transfer deficit 29, 147

treadmilling 122; see also grinding

trolling 131–132

tweens: culture of 50; and first phone 52–53; homework 152–153; and peers 48–49; tech trends for 49–52

video game addiction (VGA) 115–117

video game violence see violence in video games

violence in video games 123, 127–130

virtual reality (VR) 135–136

WhatsApp 51

WiFi: access to families 155; history of 10–11

World Health Organization (WHO) 116–118

World of Warcraft (WoW) 9, 57, 122, 134

youth developmental stages: teens 64–66; young children 27–33

YouTube: algorithm of 58; and Generation Alphas 34–35, 159; learning 159–160; marketing to children 148–149; popularity of 34; and tweens 45, 50–51; YouTube Kids 34, 58

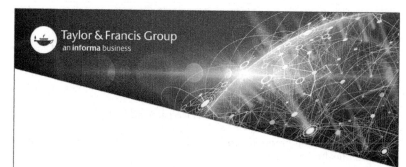

Made in the USA
Middletown, DE
25 March 2021

36246408R00116